SPOUSE ABUSE

A Treatment Program for Couples

Peter H. Neidig & Dale H. Friedman

RESEARCH PRESS COMPANY
2612 NORTH MATTIS AVENUE
CHAMPAIGN, ILLINOIS 61821

Advisory Editor, Frederick H. Kanfer

Cover design by Jack W. Davis
Composition by Omegatype

ISBN 0-87822-234-0
Library of Congress Catalog Card Number 84-61187

To the participants, past and present,
of the Domestic Conflict Containment Program

Contents

Chapter One

Introduction to the Program

The primary goal of the program is an immediate and complete cessation of violence in cases of spouse abuse. To accomplish this goal, a skill-building training format has been adopted that draws heavily on social-learning and cognitive-restructuring principles. The program does *not* focus on the past or on pathology, nor is a high level of confrontation or personal disclosure encouraged in areas unrelated to the expression of violence.

Meeting this primary goal requires clients to accept personal responsibility for their behavior and to make a sincere commitment to change. The program helps clients do this by making them aware of the factors that contribute to their involvement in violence, and improving their self-control and problem-solving abilities.

PROGRAM DEVELOPMENT

This program was developed through our work with the U.S. Marine Corps investigating the causes and correlates of spouse abuse. We began initially to interview military men who were involved in episodes of domestic violence and to administer a battery of psychological tests to them. The results of that work led us to conclude that the episodes of spouse abuse that we were investigating could be linked to specific, measurable skill deficits in the areas of anger control, stress management, and communication. The violence typically occurred in the context of a dysfunctional relationship during periods of high stress. There was no evidence among the men we worked with of a high level of individual psychopathology, and they seemed, for the most part, to be interested in trying to understand the causes of the violence and in working to eliminate it.

At the time we began to develop our program, almost all treatment programs for spouse abuse were committed to separating spouses and "rescuing" wives through the use of shelters. Treatment was generally segregated by gender and devoted to individual rehabilitation with the implicit goal of assisting the client to make a permanent break from the abusive relationship (Weitzman & Dreen, 1982). The literature also appealed for the reform of the societal forces that were presumed to be the basic cause of abuse directed at women.

The emphasis on separation and shelter seemed to be based on the assumption that women involved in abusive relationships wanted to end those relationships and that nothing short of terminating the marriage would end the violence. This assumption persisted in spite of growing evidence that most women seeking assistance for abuse reported that they would prefer to stay in the relationship if the violence could be eliminated (Geller, 1978), and that among those women going to shelters most chose to stay for only brief periods before returning to their husbands (Walker, 1979; LaBell, 1979). This discrepancy between the treatment goal envisioned by the service providers (shelter leading to permanent termination of the marriage) and the need as perceived by the clients (temporary refuge and a return to the marriage) may have contributed to the "cynicism and frustration among the professionals dealing with [battered women]" (Pfouts, 1978, pp. 101–102).

The few treatment programs that did attempt rehabilitation and a resumption of the marital relationship seemed to adopt a unilateral view of spouse abuse, in which the male was seen as the source of the violence, as opposed to a perspective in which the relationship or interpersonal factors were seen as the sources of violence. The male was presumed to be the source of the the violence either because he had internalized certain societal norms that perpetuate violence (Dobash & Dobash, 1979), or because of some individual pathology. Males involved in abusive relationships were characterized in the literature as sociopathic and impulsive (Martin, 1976), authoritarian and patriarchal (Pagelow, 1981), possessing low self-esteem (Saunders, 1982), and subscribing to certain nonegalitarian sex role stereotypes (Walker, 1979). The assumption that personality and attitudinal variables, which can be quite resistant to modification, played a primary causal role in abuse probably contributed to an assumption that treatment would need to be long-term and that the prognosis for the cessation of violence was not good. Although there may be a connection between personality and attitudinal variables and abuse in some cases, we have found measures of stress and marital adjustment to be more significant factors, especially when marital consensus, satisfaction, and cohesion are measured (Neidig, Friedman, & Collins, Note 1). These findings confirm the impression that situational and relationship variables play a substantial role in spouse abuse. It is for this reason that there is heavy emphasis on those skills dealing with coping strategies, stress management, and relationship enhancement in this program.

The tendency to reject an interpersonal orientation in favor of the male-as-perpetrator model seemed to be based on several considerations (Neidig, in press). First, there was a need to mobilize public concern and to actively refute the myth that the incidence of spouse abuse was insignificant or that the abuse was in some way the fault of the wife's "masochistic need" (Snell, Rosenwald, & Robey, 1964). Second, the impetus for treatment in this area was coming largely from the writing of those who were closely identified with the feminist movement and who shared a common analysis of the causes of spouse abuse. Third, most of the early work was based on interviews with women from abusive relationships, and it would seem reasonable to assume that women, in their efforts to organize, understand, and communicate their experiences in an abusive situation, would tend to "punctuate" events in such a way as to introduce bias into the narration. Regardless of how well intentioned the interviewer and the subject are in such circumstances, the description of events would at best be incomplete.

Whether an interpersonal or unilateral perspective of spouse abuse is adopted is determined in part by whether treatment focuses on the injuries sustained or on the conflict tactics employed as the measure of violence (Neidig, Friedman, & Collins, Note 2). "When injuries are one's primary concern, spousal violence is about the harm that men inflict on women" (Berk, Berk, Loseke, & Rauma, 1983, p. 210). On the other hand, those who have attempted to quantify the types of violent behaviors engaged in during conflict between spouses have observed that wives "maintain their rough equality with respect to violence, irrespective of whether one measures it by incidence rate, mutuality of violence, degree of severity of the violent act, or prevalence of violence at each level of severity" (Straus, 1980b, p. 686).

Thus, although there are some compelling historical and political justifications for adopting the male-as-perpetrator view of spouse abuse, our own bias has been to consistently maintain an interpersonal perspective. We assume that when violence occurs within the context of an ongoing relationship, the behavior of each individual within the relationship is contingent on the behavior of the other, and that the behavior of each can be thought of as both a cause and an effect depending on how the interactional sequence is punctuated. It has been our experience that the interpersonal perspective fosters a sense of personal responsibility and suggests the possibility of positive intervention strategies. The unilateral view of spouse abuse, with its emphasis on societal factors as causing males to be abusive, may reduce the husand and wife's sense of guilt and responsibility while increasing their feelings of helplessness. Additionally, treatment that takes the unilateral view of violence encounters the following problems that can be avoided if the interpersonal perspective is maintained. First, there is the implication that there are fixed "victim" and "perpetrator" roles. Victims may assume that they can legitimately seek retribution or punishment, which can in turn lead to additional violent attempts to settle the score. Second, if the violence sequence is punctuated too narrowly, if either party only views the incident from his own perspective, and if interactional variables are not attended to, the violence may appear as if it erupted spontaneously and is beyond the influence of both parties. This perception is a therapeutic dead end. Third, when positive relationship factors and the contribution of both spouses to the conflict escalation process are ignored, women tend to be viewed as helpless, childlike victims, thus perpetuating conditions that may contribute to additional violence. Ultimately, it is no favor to be defined as a victim.

SELECTION CRITERIA

We have found that the seriousness of the conflict tactics employed or the types or seriousness of the injuries sustained in conflict have not had much value in determining who is an appropriate candidate for this form of treatment or in predicting response to treatment. A number of clients who have inflicted serious injury on each other have responded quite well to the program, while the couples most resistant to the goal of eliminating violence have often been those who engaged in frequent, but not very serious, physical abuse.

An approach that seems to have a good deal of utility in formulating intervention strategies and in making prognostic evaluations has been what we refer to as the violence continuum. Here violence between spouses is thought of as being on a continuum, with the poles of the continuum labeled "expressive" and "instrumental." Theoretically, an individual could be located at any point between these two extremes. People who engage in expressive violence are good candidates for this program, while people engaging in instrumental violence are not.

Expressive violence is considered to be primarily an expression or function of a high level of emotional arousal. It typically occurs in the context of gradually escalating conflict between the husband and the wife. It is usually possible in cases of expressive violence to identify a precipitating event such as the violation of an implicit relationship rule and, in retrospect, to identify the sequential steps in the process of conflict escalation. Expressive violence involves the participation of each spouse, although not necessarily equally, in the process of escalation. In such cases, there is not a clear distinction between the victim and the perpetrator. Both parties see themselves as victims, responding more or less appropriately to the provocative behavior of the spouse. The violent episode is typically followed by a period of genuine remorse and sorrow; for in these situations, violent behavior is inconsistent with the couple's value system. Motivation for change and acceptance of personal responsibility is relatively high, once defenses such as denial and projection have been dealt with. Expressive violence, however, tends to become instrumental as it is repeated. It is important, therefore, to treat it. In cases of expressive violence where the couple intends to stay together and adequate attention is devoted to security measures, treatment containing the skill-building components of anger control, stress management, communication skills, and conflict containment has a favorable prognosis for eliminating violence.

Instrumental violence is the deliberate use of violence as an instrument or tool for social influence. It is almost always violence inflicted by men on women and can be accurately referred to as "wife battering." It is employed to punish or to control the behavior of the spouse. People who have witnessed or directly experienced a high level of violence in childhood are predisposed to move quickly from expressive to instrumental violence. The level of immediate provocation is low in incidents of instrumental violence and the process of escalation is rapid rather than gradual and sequential. Instrumental violence does not fit the mutual combat model. Here there are relatively fixed perpetrator and victim roles. The violent episode may later be followed by expressions of remorse, but they are shallow, manipulative, and motivated more out of selfish concerns than a genuine appreciation for the welfare of the spouse. The reinforcement that the abuser gets from his spouse's compliance when he uses violence is not offset by a high level of personal discomfort. The use of violence is incorporated into the individual's value system and there is little motivation for change. Here the appropriate intervention involves separation, shelter for the wife, and the possibility of legal sanctions as there is a high probability that the pattern of violence will continue. Table 1, The Violence Continuum, shows the characteristics of expressive and instrumental violence.

Table 1

The Violence Continuum

EXPRESSIVE VIOLENCE	INSTRUMENTAL VIOLENCE
Violence that is primarily an expression of emotion (anger, jealousy, etc.)	Violence that is used primarily as an instrument to achieve a goal
Absence of exposure to severe prior violence	History of exposure to severe violence
Mutual and reciprocal violence; victim and perpetrator roles not fixed	Unilateral violence; victim and perpetrator roles fixed
Violence in context of escalating conflict	Violence as deliberate effort to punish or control
Sequential, gradual, predictable progression to violence	Relatively sudden and rapid progression to violence
Mutual conflict, stress, frustration, and anger precede violent incident	Low provocation for violent incident
Genuine remorse and sorrow; violence inconsistent with values, belief that violence will be controlled	Shallow, manipulative remorse; violence consistent with values, resignation and hopelessness
Unpredictable, high potential for escalation and "accidental" injury	Potential for violent retaliation, homicide, or suicide
Relatively benign psychological consequences	Serious psychological consequences; helplessness, depression, low self-esteem, external locus of control
Brief, skill-building therapy with couples	Long-term therapy with individuals, separation, legal sanctions
Termed mutual combat, spouse abuse, or domestic violence	Termed battering

Until treatment is under way, it is difficult to tell if clients engage in expressive or instrumental violence and if they will benefit from the program. We admit most couples into the program but watch their progress carefully to see if they can indeed benefit from the treatment. We have also found that if clients have significant alcohol or drug problems, or sociopathic conditions as manifest in gross distortion, denial, absence of remorse, and a history of rebellious or antisocial behavior, the likelihood of the success of the program is reduced. Again, individuals with these problems can be admitted into the program if their behavior is monitored closely. In cases where clients do not respond to treatment, the therapist has a responsibility to recommend further treatment, separation, and security measures for the abused partner. The emphasis then changes from training clients to eliminate violence to protecting the abused partner.

Our studies (Friedman, Note 4) indicate that about 8 out of 10 program participants remained violence free for the postprogram period of time (6 months) they were followed. One indicator of how much benefit a client will get from this treatment has proven to be the client's level of participation in the later stages of the program. To date, all those who have engaged in serious postprogram violence maintained an uncooperative, resistive attitude throughout the treatment, and their level of involvement was in marked contrast to that of most participants.

USER CONSIDERATIONS

Our treatment model of choice is to work with couples in relatively small homogeneous groups where the emphasis is specifically focused on understanding and eliminating episodes of violence. Men whose wives do not attend the sessions either because they have temporarily returned to their families of origin or because of scheduling conflicts can be included in the group. They are able to participate in the discussion and in some of the exercises, and they profit from being exposed to the wives of others in the group. As long as about half of the wives can attend on a regular basis, the women don't seem to be inhibited by the fact that they are outnumbered. The advantages of having both male and female points of view represented seem to far outweigh any disadvantages. Again, the most benefit is derived from the program when both partners regularly attend sessions.

One of the advantages of the group approach is that group members tend to confront each other more directly and perhaps more effectively than the therapist can. The rehabilitation process seems to be accelerated through the small-group format. Another advantage is that couples are able to see that their situation is not unique because others in the group are struggling with many of the same issues that they struggle with. Group members can serve as both positive and negative examples for each other. A group setting also has the advantage of helping spouse abusers, who are often rather socially isolated and lack the ability to relate comfortably with others, to enhance their social skills. Group members will often spontaneously reach out to other members during times of crisis. They may find it easier to approach each other for help than approach the therapist. Frequently, group members continue to meet informally after treatment ends and, thus, maintain the social support function. A final advantage of group treatment is its efficient use of the therapist's time.

When this program was used in military settings, a high level of control over participants was possible. Attendance was compulsory for the active duty member and strongly encouraged for the nonmilitary spouse. About three-fourths of the participants' spouses attended regularly. Couples met in groups of approximately 15 people weekly for ten 2-hour sessions. At the time of the initial screening, participants were advised of the consequences of noncompliance, which included administrative disciplinary action and the possibility of discharge from the service. Resistance was typical in some early efforts by participants to test the system. This testing was usually followed by a high level of participation and significant positive behavior change.

Preliminary outcome studies indicate a high level of success (Neidig, Friedman, & Howell, Note 3) and support the position that voluntary participation is not a prerequisite to positive behavior change. The approach outlined in this book is directly applicable in settings where compulsory attendance can be required (such as military settings or court-mandated programs) and, with a strong commitment for participation from couples, it is applicable in voluntary settings as well.

The orientation and much of the content of the program could be applied by a therapist working with a single couple. Even though the benefits that derive from the participation in a group would be lost, they may be offset by the additional opportunity for individualized instruction. A number of therapists who have worked with our program have reported finding the material to be of use in their work with couples.

The least effective application of our approach would be in individual therapy when only one partner is available for treatment. Under those circumstances, it would be difficult to maintain a focus on the relationship, which is basic to our approach. Even so, selected portions of the text and the exercises may prove to be of some benefit.

This program has been conducted by individuals with backgrounds in education and psychology. Both groups do equally well, although they have somewhat different adjustments to make in adapting to the program format. Educators seem to be more comfortable with the structured, didactic quality of the material but may lack some experience with group processes. Therapists may have difficulty resisting the temptation to pursue issues not directly related to the issue of violence and adhere to the positive, present, skill-building orientation.

Our intent in developing this book has been to provide a thorough description of one approach to the rehabilitation of those people involved in spouse abuse. No claim is made that this is the only, or even the best, approach; however, it is our hope that the book will prove to be a useful tool for those working in this challenging field.

PROGRAM CURRICULUM

This program uses a specific core curriculum to eliminate violence. The core curriculum is designed to enable clients to:

1. Accept personal responsibility for violent behavior;
2. Contract for a commitment to change;
3. Develop and utilize time-out and other security mechanisms;
4. Understand the unique factors involved in the violence sequence;
5. Master anger-control skills;
6. Develop the ability to contain interpersonal conflict through the problem-solving process.

The following supplemental areas detailed in this book are also important in the treatment of spouse abuse, depending upon the needs of the particular client or group.

- Additional anger-control techniques such as
  - Assertion training
  - Stress-inoculation training
  - Empathy
  - Dealing with criticism
  - Focusing on the positive
- Stress-management training
- Communication skills
- Jealousy
- Sex role stereotyping
- Marital dependency
- Isolation and social support

Materials from both the core curriculum and supplemental areas have been included in this book. Far more content has been included in most chapters than could possibly be covered in one session. Users should familiarize themselves with the entire book so they can respond in a flexible manner during treatment sessions. However, it is highly recommended that the core material be covered and that material be covered in the order presented in the book. Material is arranged so that clients can practice and master individual skills (such as anger control and stress management) in the earlier sessions before learning skills that need to be practiced in a relationship (such as communication and conflict containment). The assumption is that some sense of individual competency and control is a prerequisite to mastering relationship skills. Additionally, communication skills are presented before other relationship issues, because they should be in place before addressing issues such as jealousy and sex role stereotyping.

VIOLENCE FACTORS AND PROGRAM CONTENT

A number of causal factors proposed for spouse abuse have been considered in the program. At this stage of research, any decision on the causes of spouse abuse would have to be considered largely speculative. It is almost certain that violence is multidetermined; that is, each violent episode is caused by a combination of factors rather than any single factor operating in isolation. For example, a man who has been raised to believe that his worth is measured in terms of his income, and who also believes strongly that the man should be the head of the household, will be threatened by the loss of work, particularly if his wife is employed. Any additional symbolic threat to his status might, in such a situation, elicit a violent response. We believe that a treatment program must address a number of factors including predisposing factors such as each spouse's background, violence history, and personality; precipitating factors for the incident such as unresolved disputes; and maintaining factors for the violence in the relationship such as each spouse's reaction to the violence.

It is important to be familiar with the theories and factors that have been proposed to explain spouse abuse, especially when formulating intervention strategies. Speculation about causes, though, should not detract from the primary goal of treatment. The focus of intervention efforts should, of course, continue to be positive and future oriented, expressed in terms of conditions to be changed and skills acquired. To this end, most of the factors identified as contributing to the likelihood of violence in the home are addressed in the program. Causal factors that have been identified follow.

Alcohol

The link between alcohol and spouse abuse is rather firmly established in the minds of the general public and individuals who engage in abuse, who frequently report violent episodes occurring while they have been drinking. The implication of a direct causal relationship is often made; however, the precise nature of this relationship must be carefully considered.

Coleman and Straus (Note 5) have reviewed several explanatory theories dealing with this relationship. The disinhibition theory states that alcohol has the effect of reducing the inhibiting functions of the higher brain centers on the lower, more reflexive portion of the brain. Thus, alcohol is presumed to have a direct physiological effect on the drinker that results in the release of violent, antisocial behavior. The learned behavior theory would broaden this interpretation to include psychological and contextual variables. From this point of view, the person's mood, expectations, past history with alcohol, and the environment, in addition to the chemical properties of the alcohol, are all seen as influencing the person's response. Finally, the deviance disavowal theory stresses the fact that people are well aware that their conduct while drinking will be attributed to the effects of alcohol. In this manner, alcohol can serve to excuse spouse abuse by relieving people of full responsibility for their behavior and could make violence more likely by "providing, in advance, a socially approved excuse for violent behavior" (Gelles, 1972, p. 114).

The bias assumed by this program is generally consistent with both the learned behavior theory and the deviance disavowal theory. Alcohol is frequently used by people to justify or excuse violent behavior. People don't beat their spouses because they were drinking; rather, they drink in order to beat their spouses. Careful questioning about the mood the person was in before he started drinking, the expectations he had for the outcome of the drinking episode, and the fact that he certainly does not beat his family every time he has been drinking, can serve to communicate this idea.

Undoubtedly there will be people who do have a problem with alcohol severe enough to warrant prior referral to an alcohol treatment program; however, they should also be treated for spouse abuse because it cannot be assumed that the cessation of alcohol abuse will automatically lead to the cessation of spouse abuse. In this respect, it is interesting to note that a survey by Straus, Gelles, and Steinmetz (1981) found that the significant relationship between the frequency of reported drunkenness and frequency of spouse abuse rose from 2.1 violent episodes per year for those "never drunk" to 30.8 for those reporting they were "very often drunk." The figure dropped to 17.6 for those indicating "almost always drunk." It may be that alcohol is used by this group (the "almost always drunk" group) to calm or anesthetize themselves and by more moderate drinkers to disinhibit or excuse otherwise unacceptable behaviors.

Anger-Arousing Cognitions and Labeling

Attribution theory asserts that external events themselves have no direct relationship to the arousal of anger except as mediated through the processes of appraisal, expectations, and cognitions (internal sentences). The importance of cognitive determinants in the arousal of emotions has been detailed in the works of Beck (1979), Ellis (1962), Kelly (1955), and Meichenbaum (1977). The James-Lange (James, 1884) theory of emotion asserts that how we label our own response pattern determines how we subjectively experience the emotion (i.e., "I am afraid because I am running away" or "I am angry because I am breathing rapidly and have just been threatened"). Together with the experimental work of Schacter and Singer (1962), these theories indicate the importance of internal cues as well as internal labeling.

The bulk of the anger-control content of this book is based on attribution theory. Internal beliefs and automatic thoughts that influence anger arousal are exposed, and methods for substituting a less inflammatory level of rhetoric are discussed and practiced.

Compulsive Masculinity

Talcott Parsons (1947) suggested that a link between the fear of being feminine and aggression directed toward women is established because boys are initially dependent upon and identify with their mothers, but feel that they must reject this influence to grow up to become men. Acting feminine in any way may be seen as weakness. "Compulsive masculinity" then, is the tendency to engage in excessively masculine activities prompted by a sense of insecurity over sexual identification. Parsons proposed that the number of adolescent boys who engage in weight lifting and body building, the extensive use of profanity (a masculine activity) by boys in potentially fearful situations, and the seemingly senseless violence of teenage gangs when accused of cowardice all support this theory. Tolby (1966) made the following predictions based on Parsons' formulations:

1. Boys who grow up in homes dominated by a woman (matriarchal families) are more likely to engage in violence.
2. Boys who are slow to develop adult masculine characteristics are likely to be violent.

3. Working-class youths with little access to symbolic power (status, prestige, etc.) are likely to emphasize physical toughness.

Although this hypothesis remains largely unsubstantiated at this point, it seems reasonable to assume that there is a link between a man's security in his sexuality and violence: in order to maintain a position of power, men who feel insecure or easily threatened are more likely to engage in violence.

Related to compulsive masculinity is the belief held by some men raised in a "subculture of violence" that they must respond physically if their masculinity is attacked (Wolfgang, 1958). These men may apply this norm even to their wives. Compulsive masculinity and the subculture of violence are covered in the program as norms relating to the violence sequence.

Ways of Dealing with Conflict

Conflict theory takes the position that conflict is an inevitable component of life and that it is not only expected but also essential and even beneficial in any relationship (Sprey, 1969). According to this theory, it is through conflict that adaptive change occurs. At issue, then, is not whether conflict will occur, but how conflict is dealt with (Bach, 1963).

Although there can be little doubt that some degree of conflict is inherent in marriage, Straus et al. (1981) were able to find little support for conflict theory as an explanation for intrafamily violence. In fact, they found just the opposite of what would be predicted on the basis of this approach. Couples who have a high level of conflict, but who bring their problems into the open and use reasoning and negotiation would be expected not to have to use violence. However, these couples tended to be among the most violent in their survey. Those who reported no conflict and who rarely employed reason and negotiation (the group that conflict theorists would assume were repressing the inevitable problems) had the lowest rate of violence.

The amount of conflict that couples in the Straus et al. (1981) study experienced may have had more to do with how violent they were than the way they handled the conflict. Relationships with more conflict are not necessarily healthier relationships. The unbridled expression of conflict may lead to conflict escalation and then to violence. It is for this reason that conflict-containment skills are emphasized in this treatment. This program adopts the position that some conflict is inevitable in marriage, and that when it occurs, it should be dealt with openly through constructive communication and problem-solving techniques.

Lack of Empathy

Feshbach (1964) suggested that feedback from the victim of aggression prompts empathic distress in the observer. Thus, an empathic person would be inhibited from using aggression in an instrumental fashion to influence another's behavior or to use aggression in a hostile manner to inflict injury. Although this hypothesis has received some support in experimental simulation studies and in the area of delinquent acting-out behavior (Chandler, 1973), it has not been studied in respect to spouse abuse. However, observations that spouse abusers resort to a variety of defensive distortions to minimize the degree of injury or pain they have inflicted, coupled with the observation that they often have a remarkably difficult time in shifting from their own egocentric perspective to that of their victims, give support to the importance of this variable.

Empathy has been described as the cognitive ability to assume the point of view of another or as the emotional ability to feel along with the other. It is assumed that both abilities play some part in moral development and the inhibition of violence. Training in empathic skills is included in the program in the session on additional anger-control techniques.

Loss of Childhood

One of the patterns of childhood experience that has been theoretically linked to spouse abuse is what Celia Medina (1981) has labeled "loss of childhood." This term applies to men who were expected to be overly responsible as children. Their own dependency needs went unfulfilled because they had to assume jobs or the parent role at an early age. In order to deal with these harsh experiences, they developed the ability to dissociate from their feelings. Weitzman and Dreen (1982) speculate that this dissociation may explain why many violent men are mystified by their own violence and tend to rely on alcohol to further subdue feelings. Through overreliance or denial, they block from awareness their dependency conflicts, fear of intimacy, and need to control. Emphasis in the program on recognizing and accepting feelings and reducing unrealistic sex role stereotypes may help with this problem.

Psychopathology

Theories that emphasize individual psychopathology as a causal agent would attribute violence to some internal pathology. Although it is likely that some people involved in spouse abuse may, in fact, be psychotic, have organic brain damage, or be suffering from some other serious internal defect, it would seem that this is not true for the vast majority of them or their spouses (Rounsaville, 1978). Straus (1977) estimates that approximately 3 percent of people involved in abusive relationships can be diagnosed as suffering from some serious form of psychopathology. Treatment approaches like this program that are aimed at skill building are not appropriate for this type of population.

Need to Maintain Authority

Violence is one of the tools or resources family members can use to exert influence and maintain a position of authority. Resource theory suggests that because of some of the negative consequences of the use of violence (loss of affection, respect, etc.) it will be employed only as a means of last resort when other resources have failed (Goode, 1971). Violence is more likely to be used as a resource in cases of:

1. "Status inconsistency"—when a husband, who ascribes to the value that he should be the head of the household, finds that he is not; and
2. "Role reversal"—where males and females have reversed what are traditionally considered to be the functions appropriate for their respective positions.

Evidence for the use of violence in these situations can be found in the work of Gelles (1972) and Rounsaville (1978). Bagarozzi and Wordarski (1977) have discussed a similar theory of the causes of spouse abuse in terms of exchange theory. They speculate that partners develop implicit expectations of what they consider to be a fair return for the effort they invest in the relationship. When these expectations are not realized, at least to some minimal extent, the individual is likely to engage in acts designed to settle the score. Violence is among those acts engaged in when the perceived level of exchange is inequitable.

The implications for intervention suggested by these theoretical approaches include instruction in more appropriate means for achieving status and social influence, and examining and moderating the importance of traditional sex role definitions. The communication and problem-solving skills in the program teach clients how to influence others without resorting to violence. Sex role stereotypes and their impact are also examined in the program.

Learned Violence

Violent behavior is a learned response that is acquired in the same way that any other behavior pattern is acquired and maintained. Consistent with social learning theory, this program largely rejects as casual instinctual forces or variables presumed to be entirely internal, such as a weak super ego, in favor of observable determinants operating in the person's present environment. The person's perceptions, and the cognitions and values emphasized by attribution theory, are also included in this approach.

SCREENING

Potential participants for the program are referred from law enforcement agencies, the military command, and from treatment providers such as chaplains, psychologists, and local hospitals. Each couple is interviewed conjointly using the Intake Interview prior to the first session. Other test instruments, explained later in this section, can also be administered during screening. The purpose of the screening is to:

1. Make sure that applicants meet the treatment requirements; that is, they have a substantiated history of domestic violence;
2. Identify any high-risk situations that may require intervention beyond the scope of the program;
3. Secure information that will aid in determining the treatment content and developing treatment goals.

We have administered a number of screening instruments when using this program. Therapists may wish to use some of these with their clients. The most helpful of these instruments and the factors they measure are explained in the following section.

The Intake Interview

The Intake Interview is administered during the screening in order to establish the background and violence history of clients. This is important in determining if clients are appropriate candidates for this treatment program. Only those couples who have been involved in at least one episode of serious violence, as shown on the Intake Interview, should be involved in the program, as having clients in the program who have not experienced violence tends to dilute the focus of the program. It should be clear to all clients that they are there because of their violent behavior and that the purpose of the program is to eliminate any additional episodes of violence.

The information gathered during the Intake Interview is used to consider three levels of causal factors: predisposing, precipitating, and maintaining factors. Predisposing factors are those that set the stage for violence and seem to be important in influencing how rapidly violence is likely to escalate along the violence continuum once it has occurred within the relationship. Severe levels of violence or emotional deprivation witnessed or experienced during childhood are significant predisposing variables. Precipitating factors, although not sufficient by themselves to lead to violence, may trigger a violent episode in combination with predisposing factors. Precipitating factors include behaviors that are threatening or communicate disdain, which spouses may engage in during times of high stress and conflict. Maintaining factors are behaviors that give tacit approval to the violence, perhaps by covering it up, or like the renewed feelings of intimacy couples often experience after violence, offer hope that the violence will not occur again.

The level of remorse for violent incidents and maintaining factors such as the immediate consequences for the violent act and the spouse's response to the violence are frequently underemphasized in planning intervention and predicting success. As a means of social influence, violence, in the short-term, is a remarkably effective method of securing compliance. Consequently, it tends to be reinforced by the compliance of others. In cases of expressive violence, this reinforcement is offset by the experience of genuine remorse and sorrow. Although the concept of remorse may strike some as moralistic or superficial, it has proven to be of great significance in positioning individuals on the violence continuum and thus determining the appropriate intervention strategy for the client. It is the presence of remorse and inconsistency of the violent behavior with the values and self-concept of the individual that are most indicative of expressive, rather than instrumental, violence. The ability to transcend an egocentric orientation and experience grief for the victim is not found in cases of instrumental violence. The degree of remorse is assessed during the Intake Interview by "walking through" the last violent episode with the couple and noting the extent of defensiveness and denial of responsibility.

The husband and wife are interviewed together during intake. Although this may inhibit, to some extent, the level of candor and self-disclosure initially, some loss of information is more than made up for by the following advantages:

1. The appearance of collusion between one spouse and the therapist leading to exclusion of the other spouse is reduced.
2. The idea that the treatment unit is the couple is enhanced by seeing both together and asking the same questions of both.
3. The issue of secrets (information confided by one spouse, the knowledge of which is not to be conveyed to the other) is avoided. This eliminates the problem for the therapist of dealing with such information.
4. Suspiciousness is reduced and the potential for one spouse to violently interrogate the other concerning what may have been divulged in the interview session is avoided.
5. Finally, interviewing the husband and wife together makes it clear that the therapist is not assuming responsibility for the security of the individuals. They maintain responsibility by deciding what they feel secure in revealing. The therapist does not confront or encourage premature disclosures, which might jeopardize the integrity of the relationship or place either spouse at risk.

Our Intake Interview is found in the Appendix and may be copied for use in conducting the program.

The Conflict Tactics Scale

This scale (Straus, 1979) lists the methods used in resolving conflict in ascending order of severity from the use of rational discussion, to the use of verbal abuse, physical threat, and physical abuse. We have found this questionnaire useful in quantifying the frequency and severity of violent behavior. With the husband and wife both present, we asked each to report only on his or her own behavior. Scores on this instrument for our clients indicate some gender differences in conflict behaviors with women reporting more episodes of verbal abuse and males more episodes of physical threat. However, in the area of physical abuse the scores tend to be comparable for both sexes. When multiple acts of physical abuse have occurred it is quite rare for only one spouse to report engaging in violent behaviors (Neidig, Note 6).

The Dyadic Adjustment Scale

The Dyadic Adjustment Scale (Spanier, 1976) is a 32-item scale for assessing the quality of marriage. It measures consensus—the extent of agreement on issues important to the functioning of the marriage; affectional expression—satisfaction with the level of sexual and affectionate behavior; satisfaction—the level of satisfaction and commitment to the relationship; and cohesion—the extent to which the couple engages in pleasurable mutual activities.

The level of satisfaction of a client's marriage has proven to be a predictive measure for expressive violence. Marriages of abusive couples are likely to be quite unsatisfactory and dysfunctional. We administered this scale pre- and postprogram and found that clients scored significantly higher on the scale after treatment (Neidig, Note 6).

The Locus of Control Scale

This scale (Nowicki & Marshall, 1974) is used to measure how much individuals perceive the events in their life to be a consequence of their own behavior, and therefore controllable (internal control), or as being unrelated to their own behavior and therefore beyond personal control (external control). Abusive individuals tend to perceive themselves as having little control over their behavior as measured by the scale. They are likely to blame their conduct on external factors and to avoid assuming personal responsibility. We administered this scale to clients both pre- and postprogram and found clients to score more in the external locus of control at the beginning of treatment than a military control group. The wives in treatment scored consistently more in the external locus of control than their husbands at the beginning of the program. At the end of the program, clients' scores compared favorably to the scores of the control group (Neidig, Note 6).

The Life Events Scale

This scale is a checklist of the stressful events that clients may have experienced during the past year. We used the Holmes and Rahe Social Readjustment Rating Scale (Holmes & Rahe, 1967) to develop our Life Events Scale. Scores were obtained by adding the number of items marked; high scores indicate a high-stress level. We found this to be a significant way to predict violence. A common precipitating factor for expressive violence is a high level of marital conflict that is occurring in the context of considerable stress and frustration. Our modification of the Holmes and Rahe scale showed significant differences in stress levels between abusive and nonabusive individuals (Neidig, Note 6).

The Assertiveness Scale

The Assertiveness Scale (Alberti & Emmons, 1970) is used as a measure of communication skills and assertiveness. It would appear that abusive couples are characterized by a specific deficit in the area of ability to communicate and resolve conflict without resorting to excessively passive or aggressive strategies. We used a modification of the Alberti and Emmons Assertiveness Scale to identify people who needed assertiveness training.

The Empathy Scale

This scale (Mehrabian & Epstein, 1972) is used to identify people who have a marked lack of empathy for others. Empathy-building techniques may be included in the treatment program for these people.

TRAINING APPROACH

The skill-training approach employed for this program includes three basic components: instruction, behavioral rehearsal, and feedback.

Instruction

Instruction is accomplished through the use of brief lectures, demonstrations, and films (optional). Some of the instruction provides direct information and vocabulary necessary to increase clients' self-control and repertoire of social skills. Indirect instruction, such as the role models presented by therapists, is also an important program component. For example, our groups have been conducted by both a single male leader and by male and female co-leaders. We recommend the male and female co-leader model because female group members participate more quickly with this model and because cooperative, nonsexualized modes of relating can be modeled. A male leader can act to broaden the acceptable range of masculine behaviors through modeling certain attitudes and styles of interaction and through self-disclosure. Therapists working with individual clients or couples should also be aware of the role models they provide.

Learning is facilitated by a highly structured presentation of material with clearly defined goals and small, sequentially ordered steps. Clients learn most easily when the atmosphere is emotionally neutral or positive, and when they understand the rationale for each of the program elements. If clients understand why each topic is included, both motivation and the ability to generalize the content to new situations is increased. In explaining the rationale for various segments, it is important to differentiate personal bias from positions that can be well supported empirically. For example, that domestic violence should play no part in the life of a family is a bias; however, the relationship between witnessing or experiencing serious violence during childhood and subsequent violent conduct as an adult is well documented.

To facilitate instruction, each topic in this book is prefaced with a section that includes information suitable for a brief lecture or introduction for the demonstrations, exercises, and homework assignments that follow. Additional references and resources are also cited.

Behavioral Rehearsal

In many respects, the behavioral rehearsal component of this program is the most important aspect of the skill training. Through rehearsal, clients can apply what they have learned during the instruction segments and their level of mastery can be observed. Behavioral rehearsal takes place during the exercises that are completed in session or assigned as homework.

The discussions and exercises conducted during the sessions provide an opportunity for clients to receive immediate feedback. Homework assignments, on the other hand, do not provide this opportunity, and, thus, clients are less likely to do them. The rationale for each assignment and detailed, step-by-step instructions must be given. Ask if each client understands both the rationale for the assignment and the instructions. Responses such as "I think so" and "I'll try" suggest minimal commitment and should be clarified.

Each assignment needs to be carefully monitored for compliance. If behavioral rehearsal has not been at least attempted, the rationale, instructions, and importance of the exercise should be repeated and the homework assigned again for next week. In group settings, members influence each other to participate; calling on those who are most likely to have completed their assignments will facilitate participation.

Exercises or homework assignments or both have been included for all major content areas. These provide the opportunity for behavioral rehearsal necessary to consolidate and personalize learning. They should be approached as opportunities for experimentation and growth rather than as tests demanding immediately high standards of performance. To accomplish this, attention must be focused on the feedback component. Indeed, the distinction between feedback and behavioral rehearsal often becomes blurred as one leads naturally to the next one.

Feedback

The feedback provided to clients is a critical component in the learning/behavior-change process. Feedback should be positive, specific, limited to those areas under the voluntary control of the recipient, and delivered in a manner that promotes gradual, step-by-step progress toward an agreed-upon goal.

Where negative feedback is required, it should, whenever possible, be prefaced by a positive statement. Feedback should be descriptive rather than judgmental and continually focus on the behavior of the individual; for example, "That sure was a self-defeating thing to do" rather than "Boy, are you ever stupid."

Compliance should be continually monitored and reinforced. However, in prompting desired behaviors and reinforcing their occurrence, care should be exercised not to totally dominate spontaneous interactions. Goals should be modest; the focus is to eliminate violence, not to effect sweeping personality change. Feedback should communicate acceptance and respect for the client at all times, although certain aspects of the client's behavior may be defined as clearly inappropriate, self-defeating, and in need of modification. Because an important program component is for the therapist to model desired behaviors, the feedback provided should be consistent with the skills of communication detailed in this book.

USE OF THE BOOK

Each of the following chapters corresponds to one session. More information than could be covered in a session is included in most chapters so that program users can choose material applicable to their clients. Depending upon the needs of their clients, users may wish to expand the material in some chapters to two or three sessions.

Each chapter includes:

1. Introductory material suitable for use as the basis for a brief lecture. References are included to permit users to acquaint themselves with original source material.
2. Demonstrations or exercises suitable for in-session use to develop the topic and permit opportunities for behavioral rehearsal or assignment as homework.

3. Worksheets, handouts, forms, and contracts that may be duplicated and distributed to clients. The worksheets are used in many of the in-session exercises and are also assigned as homework. Handouts summarize material presented during the session and act as prompts and learning aids for clients. Forms and contracts include self-monitoring and evaluation forms used by clients and contracts committing clients to behavior changes.

Exercises, worksheets, handouts, forms, and contracts are found at the back of each chapter. All the exercises are together followed by the material for clients, which is presented in the order that it is mentioned in the chapter.

Nine session outlines, located at the end of this chapter, highlight the presentation sequence for each session.

The masculine pronoun has been used most frequently in this text because of the difficulty in writing sexually neutral descriptions. This usage is not meant to imply that the behavior in question is engaged in only by males. We believe that expressive violence, which is responsive to our treatment approach, is best understood as a relationship issue of mutual escalation. The terms "victim" and "villain" are not particularly helpful in understanding the violence sequence and certainly neither spouse can claim exclusive right to either role.

CONDUCTING SESSIONS

Each client is given a folder during the first session and is requested to keep all material distributed in the folder and to bring the folder to each session. The use of unbound folders enables the therapist to distribute only those materials which are to be covered. In this way, the resulting selection of materials will be tailored to the needs of the clients. The materials should be selected in such a way that the core curriculum is covered as well as those supplemental materials chosen to meet the unique needs of the clients. The therapist should make specific homework assignments and be sure to inquire the following week about compliance.

Each session after the first should be started by "checking in." This includes asking clients if they have their folders with completed homework assignments, and how their week has been. Each client should be explicitly questioned concerning acts of violence or difficulty in controlling emotions and behavior. This time is both for rewarding positive behavior and establishing an agenda of issues that will require elaboration during the course of the session.

All clients need ample opportunity to raise issues they consider relevant. For those reporting an uneventful week, the response that "you must have been doing something right" will reinforce the idea that positive events are not due to luck or chance. It is as important for clients to understand what makes things go well as it is to discuss problems, for it is only in understanding what causes positive change that it can be brought under voluntary and deliberate control.

The spouse should be invited to concur or disagree with the partner's representation: "Is that how it seemed to you?" or "Do you remember it in the same way?" However, open disagreement or confrontation should be avoided if either partner seems particularly apprehensive. To avoid escalating the violence in their relationship, clients have the right to set limits on how much confrontation and disclosure they are comfortable allowing.

Underlining common issues when conducting sessions in a group will serve to increase the cohesiveness of the group: "Your experiences sound very much like. . ." or "I wonder if any of the rest of you have had similar experiences?"

In cases where clients report a violent episode, sufficient detail should be elicited to determine if the clients are assuming responsibility for their behavior. Clients' feelings of anger, which may have led to the violence, should be accepted to permit full disclosure. Evidence of any positive efforts at restraint and self-control should be reinforced and then the situation should be analyzed using the anger log format. (Anger Log I is introduced in Chapter Three and Anger Log II is introduced in Chapter Four.) The thoughts involved should be detailed and alternative ways of coping in the future discussed.

Several issues may have to be tabled in order to finish this segment in 15 to 20 minutes when working with a group. Those issues can, perhaps, be listed on the board, with assurances that they will be dealt with at some time during the session. Priority is given to covering the core material scheduled for any particular session. Whenever possible, the presentation of this material will make use of the concerns expressed by the clients and examples will be drawn from the information they volunteer during the check-in. It is probably better to err in the direction of redundancy when presenting material than to overwhelm clients with too much content. Much of the group's sense of spontaneity and relevance depends on the therapist's ability to accomplish the task of covering the course content for the particular session using the issues and experiences raised by clients as examples.

It should be noted that the content and pacing of the treatment should be responsive without being reactive. That is, a genuine interest in clients' behavior and progress needs to be conveyed and their concerns incorporated into the presentation without permitting these events to dictate the program content. It is easy to confuse talking about problems with problem resolution. The assumption is made that it is only through mastering the program's core curriculum that real progress will occur.

Homework should be assigned to clients at each session. Suggestions for homework are given in many of the session outlines. Other exercises and worksheets from the session can be assigned to clients depending on their needs.

Throughout treatment the therapist should avoid the temptation to rescue or to protect clients from the consequences of their behavior. The therapist should tolerate his own feelings of ambiguity, uncertainty, and anxiety and not insist on solutions (such as the wife going to a shelter) solely because it would make him feel better.

It is important for the therapist to be available and responsive. Abusive couples often live from one crisis to the next and will initially value the therapist in terms of what he can do for them in these situations. If the therapist needs to intervene in a dispute in the client's home, he should consider taking the police along and introducing them to the family, explaining that he was not sure if they would be needed. They can leave as soon as the therapist feels secure. By asking the wife to make some coffee, the therapist can separate the couple and redefine the call along social lines.

SESSION 1 OUTLINE

BEGINNING THE PROGRAM

The material for this session is found in Chapter Two.

In group sessions, introduce group leaders and clients asking everyone to share his name, how long he has been married, and number and ages of his children.

Distribute workbook folders to each client containing all handouts, worksheets, and contracts for Session 1.

Discuss program goals by reviewing the program principles. Give clients the Program Principles Handout and encourage them to make notes and ask questions during the discussion.

Outline the core content of the program, housekeeping duties, such as time and place of sessions and what clients should do if they will be late, and consequences for nonattendance.

Explain and have clients sign the Client's Contract. The requirement of confidentiality for group members may require some elaboration. Collect the contracts so that a copy may be made for filing.

Discuss resistance, anxiety, and doubt. Give clients the Attitude Survey Handout.

Discuss with clients the importance of accepting responsibility for their behavior. Review the function of defense mechanisms.

Ask for a specific, detailed description of each client's last violent episode. Prompt full disclosure by referring to screening information from the Intake Interview.

Conduct and discuss Exercise 1, Self-description, using the Self-description Worksheet and formulate individual treatment goals for clients.

Discuss the importance of time-out. Have clients complete and sign the Time-out Contract.

SESSION 2 OUTLINE

UNDERSTANDING VIOLENCE

The material for this session is found in Chapter Three.

Check in by making sure that each client has his folder and inquiring about any episodes of violence.

Return the original of the Client's Contract, keeping a copy to file.

Discuss the three-phase violence cycle. Conduct Exercise 2, The Violence Cycle, using the Violence Cycle Worksheet.

Discuss violence and anger in childhood and assign the Anger Lessons Worksheet or assign as homework.

Assign the Anger Log I as homework asking clients to record all incidents of anger they experience during the coming week.

SESSION 3 OUTLINE

ANGER CONTROL

The material for this session is found in Chapter Four.

Check in.

Review homework assignments. Make sure that clients maintained the Anger Log I for the week and reinforce positive compliance.

Explain the A-B-C theory of emotional arousal. Conduct Exercise 3, Turning It Upside Down, and Exercise 4, Attribution.

Return to incidents from the Anger Log I homework, and detail them using the A-B-C model.

Discuss cognitive distortions and irrational beliefs.

Discuss identifying and refuting automatic thoughts. Conduct Exercise 5, Hot Words. Assign the A-B-Cs of Anger Control Self-analysis Worksheet as homework.

Discuss the advantages and disadvantages of anger. Conduct Exercise 6, The Double Column Technique. Ask clients to continue to record incidents of anger using the Anger Log I from Chapter Three, unless they have mastered identifying irrational thoughts and are ready to refute them. The Anger Log II may be assigned in that case.

SESSION 4 OUTLINE

ADDITIONAL ANGER-CONTROL TECHNIQUES

The material for this session is found in Chapter Five.

Check in.

Review homework assignments. Make sure that clients have been continuing to maintain the Anger Log I (or II) for the week and reinforce positive compliance.

Use incidents from the client's anger logs to review the A-B-C model of emotional arousal.

Discuss assertion training. Give clients the Nonassertive, Assertive, and Aggressive Behavior Handout. Conduct Exercise 7, the Bill of Rights, which uses the Bill of Rights Worksheet, and Exercise 8, Assertiveness Practice.

Discuss stress-inoculation training. Distribute the Anger Management Self-statements Handout.

Discuss empathy. Conduct Exercise 9, Empathy.

Discuss dealing with criticism. Conduct Exercise 10, Dealing with Criticism.

Discuss avoiding anger pollution, humor, expecting craziness, rewriting the rules, and focusing on the positive.

Have clients record all incidents of anger on the Anger Log II from Chapter Four for the coming week.

SESSION 5 OUTLINE

STRESS AND VIOLENCE

The material for this session is found in Chapter Six.

Check in.

Review the Anger Log II and reinforce clients for positive compliance.

Discuss the measurement of stress and the intervening variables in stress and violence.

If appropriate, review the military stressors and conduct Exercise 11, The Good Soldier Versus the Good Husband/Parent.

Introduce stress-management training.

> Discuss identifying stress symptoms and the effects of stress on the body. Conduct Exercise 12, Stress Symptom Generation, using the Stress Symptoms Handout.

> Discuss identifying stressors. Conduct Exercise 13, Stressor Identification, using the Irrational Beliefs Handout.

> Discuss developing a plan and acquiring skills to deal with stressors and implementing plan.

Introduce clients to relaxation training as a method of stress control. Conduct Exercise 14, Relaxation.

Assign the Anger Log II from Chapter Four and relaxation practice as homework.

SESSION 6 OUTLINE

COMMUNICATION

The material for this session is found in Chapter Seven.

Check in.

Review the Anger Log II and reinforce positive compliance.

Conduct a brief relaxation procedure using the Relaxation Script from Chapter Six or the deep-breathing instructions from Chapter Four.

Introduce the communication principles.

> Discuss the idea that the message sent and received may differ. Conduct Exercise 15, Message Sent and Message Received.

> Discuss the impossibility of not communicating. Conduct Exercise 16, It Is Impossible Not to Communicate.

> Discuss the content and feeling components of a message. Conduct Exercise 17, Content and Feeling Components.

> Discuss how nonverbal cues are more believable than verbal ones. Conduct Exercise 18, Nonverbal and Verbal Cues.

Introduce the communication skills.

> Discuss listening. Conduct Exercise 19, Precondition for Listening.

> Discuss validation. Conduct Exercise 20, Validation.

> Discuss feeling-talk. Conduct Exercise 21, Socialization, and Exercise 22, Getting to Know Your Feelings, using the Feelings List Handout. Assign Exercise 23, Feeling-talk, as homework.

> Discuss positive expression. Conduct Exercise 24, Positive Expression, using the Positive Expressions Handout.

SESSION 6 (cont.)

Discuss negative feeling expression. Conduct client role plays.

Discuss request making. Conduct Exercise 25, Request Making.

Discuss evaluating and developing their communication skills with clients. Conduct Exercise 26, Practicing and Evaluating Communication, using the Communication Prompting and Evaluating Worksheet.

Assign the Anger Log II from Chapter Four as homework. Assign additional homework from exercises if desired.

SESSION 7 OUTLINE

THE INEVITABILITY OF CONFLICT

The material for this session is found in Chapter Eight.

Check in.

Review the Anger Log II and other homework assignments.

Conduct a brief relaxation procedure, if needed, using the Relaxation Script from Chapter Six or the deep-breathing instructions from Chapter Four.

Review any communication material left over from Session 6.

Discuss the sources of family conflict. Conduct Exercise 27, Conflict Issues Survey, and Exercise 28, Treating Family Like Strangers.

Introduce approaches to conflict.

> Discuss conflict orientation, conflict tactics, and conflict escalation. Conduct Exercise 29, Conflict Escalation, using the Conflict Escalation Handout.

Discuss conflict containment. Give clients the Conflict Containment Principles Handout and encourage them to make notes and ask questions during the discussion. Conduct Exercise 30, Dirty Fighting Techniques, using the Dirty Fighting Techniques Handout. Distribute the Dirty Fighting Score Sheet if needed as a prompt or to score couples.

Assign Exercise 31, Applying Skills, using the Communication Prompting and Evaluating Worksheet from Chapter Seven and the Conflict Containment Principles Handout as homework. Assign additional homework from exercises if desired.

SESSION 8 OUTLINE

JEALOUSY, SEX ROLE STEREOTYPING, AND MARITAL DEPENDENCY

The material for this session is found in Chapter Nine.

Check in.

Review homework assignments.

Conduct a brief relaxation procedure, if needed, using the Relaxation Script from Chapter Six or the deep-breathing instructions from Chapter Four.

Discuss the fact that this is the next to last session. Invite clients to raise any unfinished business.

Introduce the topic of jealousy.

> Discuss issues in the treatment of jealousy. Conduct Exercise 32, Putting Primary Emotions into Words; Exercise 33, Jealousy Role Reversal; and Exercise 34, Exercising Control.

> Discuss intervention strategies. Have clients record all incidents of jealousy on the Anger Log II from Chapter Four for the coming week.

Introduce the topic of sex role stereotyping. Conduct Exercise 35, Sex Role Characteristics.

> Discuss sexuality. Conduct Exercise 36, Sex Attitudes, using the Sex Attitude Worksheet.

> Discuss the ideas of dominance in marriage and decision making. Conduct Exercise 37, Decision Making, with the Decision Making Worksheet.

Introduce the topic of marital dependency. Conduct Exercise 38, Why Stay? and Exercise 29, Imagining Alternatives to Marriage.

> Discuss contingency plans. Conduct Exercise 40, Contingency Plans, using the Contingency Contract.

Assign homework from exercises if desired.

SESSION 9 OUTLINE

CLOSING THE PROGRAM

The material for this session is found in Chapter Ten.

Check in.

Review homework assignments.

Discuss isolation and social support. Conduct Exercise 41, Strengthening Social Support, using the Support Network Evaluation Worksheet.

Review and summarize relevant program principles and content. Discuss the consequences of continued violence.

Have clients complete and discuss the Maintaining Your Gains form.

Have clients fill out the Client's Evaluation.

Chapter Two

Beginning the Program

The first session of treatment presents the program principles to clients and helps them reduce resistance to treatment. It also explores defense mechanisms that prevent them from taking personal responsibility for their violent behavior, formulates treatment goals, and sets in place a time-out procedure to interrupt any violent episodes.

PROGRAM PRINCIPLES

The following principles constitute the beliefs or biases on which the program is founded. The principles need to be clearly and consistently represented to clients to orient them and make them more aware of the relevance of each program component. Stating the principles leads clients to adopt a conceptualization of abuse that helps them assume personal responsibility for their behavior and think in terms of positive change strategies (Margolin, 1979). Whenever possible, care should be taken to clearly label what are biases, or value-based positions, and what portions of the principles and program are factual or relatively value free (Stuart, 1980b) because clients have a right to know the distinction. Additionally, by taking the effort to clearly articulate the principles, the therapist will become clear about what assumptions he is making about spouse abuse. When this is not done, the therapist may be continually struggling to assess each new issue with which he is confronted. For example, by adopting the consistent stance that violence is never justified, the therapist avoids having to examine each episode presented by the clients. Or, by choosing to consistently define violence in relationship terms, the therapist will not be tempted to analyze a new episode in terms of whose fault it is. The principles underlying the program are:

1. The primary goal of the program is to eliminate violence in the home. This goal takes precedence over any other consideration. It is to this goal that the program is directed, and it is for this reason that the various program components are included. The individual skill-building and relationship-enhancement exercises are included not as ends in themselves, but because it is assumed that they will help to eliminate violence.

The importance of eliminating violence can be underscored by reviewing the fact that violence breeds violence. Children who have been subjected to violence or witnessed it in the home are more likely to engage in violent behavior themselves as they grow up and are more likely to abuse their own children (Straus, 1977). Despite the clients' conviction that each episode will be the last (the "ray-of-hope" phenomenon), violence, if untreated, tends to escalate in both frequency and intensity. The consequences of the escalation of violence are quite serious—a person is much more likely to be killed or seriously impaired by a family member at home than by a stranger elsewhere (Mulvihill, Tumin, & Curtis, 1969). Most homicide victims know their assailant, and about half of all homicides occur during the course of an argument (Tyler, 1983). These findings underscore the importance of improving interpersonal relationships, particularly between family members, and the critical importance of conflict-containment skills.

It should be understood that the intent of the program is *not* to preserve relationships at any cost, although most participants in the program reported a significant increase in marital satisfaction (Friedman, Note 4). Clients should develop contingency plans if necessary for separating, either temporarily or permanently, to protect themselves or the children, and the conditions under which the plans will be implemented should be clear to all parties. These plans, and the availability of alternate resources (shelters, etc.), reduce the extreme marital dependency that often serves to perpetuate domestic violence (Yllo, Note 7). A well-reasoned, deliberate decision to responsibly terminate a relationship should not be considered a program failure.

2. Although anger and conflict are normal elements of family life, violence in the family is never justified. It is assumed that all family members have the right to live without fear and that even a single episode of violence can have far-reaching consequences in upsetting the balance of conditions essential for optimal growth. The marriage license is not a hitting license.

In presenting this principle, feelings should be clearly distinguished from behavior and it should be established that no behavior justifies a response of violence. There may, however, be some need for clients to discuss what constitutes violence for them and for the therapist to participate actively in this process. For example, we accept the fact that whether or not we approve, the vast majority of clients believe that it is their responsibility to use physical punishment when dealing with their children. Under these circumstances, the therapist may choose to focus on the more serious forms of domestic violence by disregarding certain behaviors that, although technically violent, would be beyond the scope of the program to appreciably influence. Not to threaten or commit violence against any member of their family is a goal for clients to strive for throughout the program. However, subsequent episodes of violence are responded to as regrettable, but not altogether unexpected, events. Any agreed upon consequences are carried out in a nonpunitive manner.

3. Abusiveness is a learned behavior. Frequently, both the husband and the wife assume that violent behavior is caused by factors that are beyond their ability to control. When abuse is conceptualized in terms of a disease process, heredity, or a personality defect, both are relieved of responsibility and positive change is unlikely. Clients need to identify the steps in their own violence sequence, that is, the stressors that contribute to violence, the cues of rising anger, the "triggers" or specific stimuli that elicit violence, and the signs of remorse. In this program, violence and anger will be viewed as behaviors that can be understood and controlled by the client.

4. Abusive behavior is a relationship issue, but it is ultimately the responsibility of the male to control physical violence. The definition of abuse as a mutual problem is perhaps the most subtle and controversial of the program principles. Those investigators who have considered abuse from the feminist perspective have tended to describe the violence as a surprising, unpredictable act inflicted on the female victim (Walker, 1979). This approach leads to intervention strategies that involve removal of the wife from the relationship, shelters for the wives, and punishment or individual treatment for the husbands.

An approach that attributes total responsibility to either party leads to blaming, which compounds the problems. In blaming the abuser, the stage is set for the victim to demand punishment or retribution which will, in turn, lead to additional efforts by the abuser to settle the score. Blaming the victim is equally counterproductive. It is often assumed that women who stay in abusive relationships must deserve or even like to be abused. In an effort to avoid feeling helpless, women will often participate in defining themselves as the cause of the abuse. As long as they believe that their behavior prompted the violence, they feel that they can prevent its reoccurrence. Blaming is frequently a problem for the therapist as well. Shapiro (1984), in describing the reactions experienced by therapists involved in treating violent couples, observed that they initially experienced fear, anger, and disapproval of the husband and pity and concern for the wife. After one or two sessions, there would be a shift in which the man was perceived more sympathetically and the wife was seen more negatively. By the third session, Shapiro reported that therapists in his treatment setting were usually able to see both the husband and wife as "equally culpable and victimized. That is, the husband was no longer seen as a gratuitous victimizer, nor was the wife seen simply as a provocateur. During the course of treatment, the therapist repeatedly experienced an inclination to side with one or the other partner" (p. 120). It is our assumption that those therapists who have not thoroughly examined their own biases and adopted a consistent conceptual model of spouse abuse are particularly susceptible to this tendency to ascribe blame.

To avoid blaming either party, couples must think of the causes of violence in a circular feedback model rather than a linear one. When people think in linear terms of A causing B causing C causing D, they will be likely to attribute blame depending on how they punctuate the sequence (Watzlawick, Beavin, & Jackson, 1967). However, by adopting the feedback model, clients can assess their participation in a process where they are both abuser and victim. For example: when she begins to raise an issue of importance to her, he begins to feel defensive and to retreat; she in turn speaks more loudly to break through, and he retreats further to avoid the unpleasantness; she becomes more insistent and moves closer, while he begins to signal that he needs space and time to cool off; she experiences this as additional rejection and a lack of concern, and so on. Circular feedback, as opposed to linear interpretations ("Her nagging made me retreat" or "His retreat made me nag"), lends itself to constructive interventions in the escalation process, permitting each partner to accept a portion of the responsibility. Describing escalation as a process in which the individual's efforts to make things better make them worse (i.e., his ignoring to permit her to calm down) can be introduced to help clients understand how they both may come to feel victimized.

Finally, assigning ultimate responsibility to the male for controlling violence is simply recognition of the fact that both parties are not equal in physical strength. Although husband abuse does occur, the vast majority of serious injuries are sustained by wives (Berk, Berk, Loseke, & Rauma, 1983). The male's superior physical strength requires that he take responsibility should violence occur. Additionally, in assigning the final responsibility to the male, we are simply representing reality as it currently exists within the legal system. That is, if a couple were to come to the attention of the authorities for a domestic disturbance, it is unlikely that the judge would ascribe to our circular or relationship model of causation; rather, blame for the violence would be attributed to one party, and in the vast majority of situations, that party will be the male. It is not so much a question of fairness or validity but of fact that when violence comes to the attention of authorities and legal action is taken, in all likelihood, the male will be held responsible.

5. *Abusiveness is a desperate but ultimately maladaptive effort to effect relationship change.* When weighing whether or not the use of violence is maladaptive, it is necessary to distinguish between short-term and long-term consequences. In the short term, violence can be a remarkably effective means of influencing the behavior of others; giving in to the impulse to engage in violence can be quite satisfying. However, the long-term consequences of violence are almost always negative. The immediate compliance of others is usually followed by fear, anger, and behaviors intended to "settle the score."

Violence is often a manifestation of stress that occurs in a relationship where the partners have specific skill deficits. These couples often have difficulty articulating their feelings and expressing conflict issues in terms that lead to solving problems constructively. Lacking skills to achieve objectives through more appropriate means increases the likelihood of violence. Clients should understand that this is the rationale for including communication, problem solving, and conflict containment skill-building components into the program.

6. *Abusiveness tends to escalate in severity and frequency if not treated.* In addition to analyzing the violence sequence to discover those behaviors that elicit violence, the maintaining or reinforcing factors should also be explored. Violent behavior that may have occurred primarily as a function of emotion (anger, frustration, fear, etc.) is considered to be expressive as opposed to instrumental violence which is used to accomplish some goal (Steinmetz & Straus, 1974). Expressive violence tends to be repeated and to take on instrumental qualities because it is reinforced. That is, engaging in violence can be an effective method of getting your way, at least in the short run.

Another reinforcing element is the sense of tension relief and even renewed closeness frequently reported by both husband and wife following a violent outburst. Again, it is important for couples to identify these reinforcing variables and to explore alternative methods of achieving the same ends.

The Program Principles Handout lists the program principles for clients. The handout can be used for taking notes during presentation of the principles. The Client's Contract affirms understanding of program objectives and willingness to comply with the program. The handout and the contract are found in the back of the chapter after Exercise 1, along with the other client handouts, contracts, and worksheets.

RESISTANCE

Initial resistance to treatment by clients is to be expected and should be dealt with in the first session. How well resistance is handled can have much to do with how quickly a group works together and clients progress through the program.

Resistance should be considered a natural phenomenon to be accepted and worked with, rather than opposed. Sometimes minor manifestations of resistance should simply be ignored by paying attention to clients who are more highly motivated. It is very common for those who are intially most vocal in their opposition to quickly become active participants. Some people may simply need to express their opposition and test the limits before complying fully.

Another way to approach resistance is to point out that everybody probably is somewhat reluctant to participate in treatment at first, and then discuss some of the possible sources of resistance. Some of these sources may include:

1. Resentment. No one likes being told what to do. The natural reaction is to dig in and resist this type of interference.

2. Skepticism. People have an investment in maintaining the status quo for several reasons. First, no matter how unpleasant, it is at least predictable. Change always involves risk and uncertainty. Second, people usually justify their behavior by convincing themselves that they could not have acted other than as they did. And, finally, clients may feel that if their spouse changes in a positive direction, they may be forced to change also.

Skepticism should not be met with any guarantees, but by urging clients to suspend their doubts temporarily and adopt an attitude of experimentation. "Maybe it won't work, but we won't *know* until we have tried." It may be of benefit to mention the self-fulfilling prophecy: if you remain absolutely convinced that nothing will change, you most certainly will be right.

3. Pride. It is not easy for people even to admit to themselves that they made mistakes.

4. Embarrassment. If it's hard to admit it to themselves, it's even more difficult to talk about it to others. There is also a strong feeling that "a man's home is his castle," and that he shouldn't be expected to reveal what goes on within the family.

5. Hopelessness or defeat. The "learned helplessness" theory suggests that people may adapt to a situation over which they feel they have no control by becoming apathetic, defeated, and hopeless. This, and the fear that active participation will be viewed as betrayal and result in additional violence, are among the most common sources of resistance expressed by women. The legitimacy of these concerns must be respected and assurances made that they will not be pressured into any action that is likely to increase their danger.

6. Anger. Anger is often directed at treatment received prior to entering the program. Often it is stated that, "I'm not mad at you, but at. . ." It is important to acknowledge that, particularly from the clients' point of view, they may have been dealt with unfairly by law enforcement officers or other authorities. Accepting these complaints and moving ahead is more productive than defending these targets of irritation.

The positive form of the program and the fact that clients are treated with dignity and respect throughout the program helps to reduce resistance. Again, the initial resistance tends to subside rather dramatically once clients discover that they will not be blamed (although they will be expected to assume responsibility for their behavior) and that, except for the first session, the focus will be on the future and not the past. Also, material is presented as an alternative and, perhaps, more effective way for participants to get their needs met and not moralistically as something they must do.

In settings where treatment is voluntary, more attention should be paid initially to securing a commitment for full participation. The therapist should candidly discuss the fact that in the beginning, individuals may experience a strong tendency to indulge themselves in a "flight into health." They may attempt to convince themselves that they have received maximum benefits from their treatment and attempt to terminate prematurely. If they are able to control their violent outbursts for several weeks, as most clients can, they may fail to see the relevance of participation in the entire program of skill-building components, which are presumed to be essential for maintaining a violence-free home over time.

In addition to anticipating and discussing these manifestations of resistance, which are likely to occur when external contingencies are not employed, the therapist may wish to engage in a form of contingency contracting. An example drawn from the habit reversal literature would be to have the client write a check for a donation to be made to his least favorite cause, which should be mailed by the therapist in the event that the client failed to follow through with his commitment.

Generally, never attack resistance head on, or try to argue a client out of it. Resistance is to be expected at first and will only become troublesome if the client actively works to keep it operative over the course of treatment. It can be pointed out that although few people ever volunteer or report that they need treatment, most clients involved with this program have reported on their final evaluation forms that the program was both valuable and enjoyable (Friedman, Note 4).

We found that about 3 percent of clients continued to manifest a high level of defensiveness and resistance throughout the program, adopting a passive, sullen attitude and refusing to enter into discussions (Friedman, Note 4). Thus far, all of the subsequent acts of serious violence have been committed by members of this group. It may be that this extreme form of resistance will in fact be the best predictor of recidivism.

The Attitude Survey Handout can be reviewed to help clients deal with their feelings of resistance.

DEFENSE MECHANISMS

It is very important in the treatment of spouse abuse that clients accept personal responsibility for their behavior. Defense mechanisms play a central role in enabling them to avoid this responsibility.

Clients appear to be genuinely remorseful and ashamed of their abusive behavior and yet continue to engage in it. The obvious question is why people continue to engage in behaviors that they believe to be wrong. Sykes and Matza (1957), in a thoughtful article on the causes of juvenile delinquency, pointed out that social norms are seldom expressed as categorical imperatives. Rather, these values are stated as qualified, or flexible, guides for action. In the criminal justice system this flexibility is found in such concepts as mitigating circumstances, and pleas of insanity or self-defense. Typically, these justifications, or defenses, are thought to be employed by people to rationalize or justify their conduct after the fact, thereby enabling them to maintain their self-esteem. Sykes and Matza (1957) suggest that the process of rationalization also precedes the deviant behavior, neutralizing those social controls that would otherwise inhibit the unacceptable conduct. This insight seems to have considerable relevance to the abusive situation and to the perpetuation of violence.

In the case of spouse abuse, an abusive individual generally accepts the norm that defines violence against family members as inappropriate. But, the inhibiting effect of this value is neutralized through the use of defense mechanisms, thus permitting violence to occur. It is in this way that the individual is able to genuinely perceive himself to be "more sinned against than sinner," maintain his sense of being victimized, and neutralize the otherwise potentially inhibiting effects of disapproval by self and others. This rationalization sets the stage for the cycle of violence to continue. This formulation is consistent with the finding (Friedman, Note 8) that abusive males, prior to treatment, tend to score around or above the norm on measures of self-esteem while scoring considerably in the external direction on a measure of locus of control (indicating a feeling of lack of control and responsibility for what happens to them).

The obvious implication is that the influence of defensive operations must be reduced and the assumption of personal responsibility enhanced if the cycle of violence is to be positively changed.

Examples of defense mechanisms and how they may be used by clients include:

1. Denial. This defense is the most primitive. It involves the attempt to deal with unpleasant realities by simply ignoring or refusing to acknowledge their existence. Clients may insist that well-documented events simply did not occur, that they can't remember, or that "that just wasn't me." The denial may involve the event, the sense of personal responsibility or intent, or the extent of injury. Often, both husband and wife seem to deny the seriousness of the situation, insisting that it won't happen again and that their differences have been resolved.

2. Repression. In the case of repression, the painful memories are actually excluded from awareness rather than remembered but denied. This process can be thought of as selective remembering where the person is amnesiac with regard to certain events. Often the person who was more seriously injured can recall abusive events in painful detail, vividly recalling the scene as if it were occurring to someone else and in slow motion, while the narrative of the person who inflicted the injury appears fragmented and unclear, often with gaps that cannot be reconstructed.

The distinction between denial and repression, that is, what is really forgotten and what is merely reported as forgotten is not as important as the basic principle "We are what we do." Motives or intentions are much less significant than behaviors. Usually, by working with the material that the client presents and by discussing in some detail what preceded and immediately followed the repressed portion, the existence of the problem and a sense of personal involvement can be established.

3. Projection. Here all the responsibility for the behavior is projected, or transferred, to another. Blaming the victim is quite common and involves a shift in roles so that the abuser is defined as the nonresponsible victim of the other's actions. "She made me hit her,"

"It was her fault," "She knows not to," "She hit me first" are all examples of this process of projection. Blame can also be shifted to fate, bad luck, alcohol, or job stress.

Often, by asking the client to explain exactly how "she made you hit her," the projection can be reduced. The role of alcohol is dealt with by backing up in the narrative to a point where the client is willing to assume responsibility. Ask at what point he decided to go drinking, to get drunk, to come home late, and what his feelings and intentions were when making each decision. The role of alcohol as a causal factor is generally exaggerated. Showing that the client got drunk in order to hit his spouse, instead of hit her because he was drunk, reintroduces the element of personal responsibility. For those who avoid responsibility by claiming they lost control, the selective nature of this absence of control can be pointed out by asking why they didn't kill or much more seriously injure their spouses if they were truly out of control.

4. Displacement. In displacement, there is a shift of emotion away from the individual or situation that was originally frustrating to another. This process often plays a role in the choice of the target of abuse; instead of punching his boss or commanding officer, the husband displaces his anger to a member of his family. He takes his frustrations out on his wife who, in turn, takes it out on their child, who then takes it out on a sibling or pet.

Frequently, by the time treatment begins, both partners will have shifted the focus of attention from their own behavior to the behavior of those who have intervened. This displacement can be directed toward the neighbors who may have initiated the complaint, to the police who intervened, or to the treatment program staff. It is important not to defend those who intervened as the validity of the clients' complaints is not an issue. The original abusive incident should not be lost from view.

5. Undoing. Undoing (atonement) is intended to negate unacceptable behavior. Apologizing, repenting, and asking for forgiveness are all efforts to wipe the slate clean and start over. Clients employing this defense may insist that they are not in need of treatment. However, repeating the assumption that good intentions are not sufficient to halt abusive behavior and that certain skills must be acquired and implemented will usually elicit their cooperation.

Self-disclosure and Defense Mechanisms

Clients can be encouraged to assume an increased sense of responsibility and control over their anger and violent behavior by having them describe in detail their last violent episode. This is in many respects the most awkward and painful segment of the rehabilitation process for both the therapist and the clients. It is, however, an essential component for it is only through clients' responses to detailed questioning about their violent behavior that the level of personal responsibility can be determined and reinforced. A videotaped demonstration of this portion of the program is available from: The Educational Television Endowment of South Carolina, PO Box 22575, Columbia, SC 29222. In a group setting, it is helpful to choose one of the clients judged during initial screening to be candid and open, and to then use intake data to prompt the client into full disclosure of the violent incident.

This will be the first time most clients have publicly disclosed information about violence in their homes. Care should be taken to communicate respect for their feelings while continuing to define the violent behavior as unacceptable. Preface invitations to disclose violent history with a discussion of defense mechanisms. This discussion acknowledges the need to find a balance between painful self-disclosure and the need to preserve self-esteem. Questions should be asked matter-of-factly with an attitude of inquiry and acceptance. It's important to be neither too confrontative (stirring up painful content and mobilizing defenses and resistance) nor too accepting (suggesting gullibility and permitting clients to continue to avoid personal responsibility).

Defense mechanisms should not be labeled or, in most cases, directly confronted when clients describe their incidents of abuse, but clients should be encouraged to assume as much responsibility for their behavior as they are capable of assuming. Questioning about specific details ("How many times did you strike her?" "Where?" "Open or closed fist?") will tend to establish a sense of responsibility. Evidence that the violence was selective (i.e., hitting where bruises would not be evident, avoiding witnesses, injuring but not killing her) will reinforce the idea that the abuser's conduct was, to a considerable extent, deliberate and under voluntary control.

Through the process of self-disclosure, the "fallacy of uniqueness" (that is, the clients' perception that they are alone or unique in their experience of violence) will be reduced. A realistic sense of optimism that change is possible should be engendered. Issues raised in clients' narratives (jealousy, insecurity, control, parenting concerns, etc.) should be emphasized and considered in the future. The issues identified when the clients are describing their last violent episode are simply noted at this point and the clients are informed as to when in the course of treatment they will be discussed. For example, if a couple began fighting because of jealousy, they would be told that jealousy will be covered after there has been some opportunity to talk about communication and conflict containment and the chance to practice these skills on "easier" topics. This idea of dealing with issues sequentially, starting with more basic skills, lets them know that they have been heard and that their concerns are legitimate, but that the issue cannot be dealt with productively at this point.

BEHAVIORS AND SKILL LEVELS
RELATED TO TREATMENT GOALS

Knowing the behaviors and skill levels of abusive couples can be helpful in deciding which areas to emphasize in treatment. This section discusses the characteristics of abusive couples found in the literature, deals with helping clients examine their own characteristics, and examines how these apply to a treatment plan.

Any description of the typical male involved in spouse abuse would have to be considered quite speculative. A number of characteristics are frequently found in the literature, but for the most part they have not been empirically validated. We have found abusive males to be somewhat rigid, authoritarian, and controlling individuals who tend to view others in a suspicious, guarded fashion. They are likely to have experienced or witnessed violence as children and report extremely high levels of stress (Neidig, in press; Friedman, Note 8). Clinical observations reported in the literature (Walker, 1981) usually suggest that the males are quite jealous, dependent, and possessive. They often have few close relationships and rely solely on their spouses to fulfill their needs for affiliation and intimacy. Typically, they have difficulty in identifying or expressing their emotions and exhibit a tendency to be critical and demanding. Any state of emotional arousal may be expressed as anger. Impulsivity, low frustration tolerance, and a tendency to overreact to minor provocation or to engage in self-defeating behavior is common (Ganley & Harris, Note 9). A high level of job frustration and excessive use of alcohol may also be part of the profile.

The existing literature on abused women describes them as low in self-esteem and self-confidence, shy, and suspicious, with a tendency to withdraw from interpersonal contact. For those involved in seriously abusive situations, apathy, depression, confusion, indecisiveness, and a rather profound level of self-doubt are often found. They may be quite dependent on their spouses and fearful of outside involvement. Often abused women ascribe to very traditional values concerning marriage and the home. Self-worth may be closely tied to identity as a wife and mother (Walker, 1983).

Again, it is important to emphasize that although personal traits may be important causal factors in some cases of spouse abuse, we have found situational and relationship variables to be more important factors (Neidig, Friedman, & Collins, Note 1). It is important, though, to help clients assume "ownership" of their behaviors and characteristics where appropriate, emphasizing that behaviors can be changed and skills learned. Exercise 1, Self-description, using the Self-description Worksheet, has proven to be effective for this purpose. Information about personal traits and behaviors elicited in discussion is also used, along with information from the Intake Interview and other screening instruments, in formulating treatment goals. Table 2, Behaviors and Skill Levels Related to Treatment Areas, lists some of the variables that therapists should consider when formulating a treatment approach and assessing progress in treatment. The table lists negative, neutral, and positive behaviors and skill levels for program treatment areas. A couple's current level of functioning for each factor can be estimated, areas in which functioning is negative can be identified, and individualized treatment goals can be developed.

Table 2
Behaviors and Skill Levels Related to Treatment Areas

	NEGATIVE	NEUTRAL	POSITIVE
PERSONAL RESPONSIBILITY	Distorts, projects, minimizes. External locus of control, no remorse.	Sees self as reactive and possessing only limited responsibility.	Accepts and expresses personal responsibilities. Internal locus of control.
ANGER/ IMPATIENCE	Criticizes, picks fights, and overreacts to frustration. Temper outbursts, rage.	Uses time-out, identifies anger-arousing thoughts, articulates feelings.	Demonstrates anger control. Recognizes voluntary control over feelings and behavior.
STRESS/ TENSION	Has stress-related disorders. Driven, perfectionistic, unable to unwind.	Recognizes stress symptoms and stressors. Acknowledges limits.	Demonstrates mastery of stress-management techniques. Makes life-style adjustment.

Table 2 (cont.)

	NEGATIVE	NEUTRAL	POSITIVE
COMMUNICATION	Criticizes. No exchange of positive content. Negative or nonverbal communication.	Discusses positive and negative content.	Demonstrates communication skills. Uses self-disclosure, and "I" statements.
CONFLICT CONTAINMENT	Personalizes. Cool, impersonal behavior or rapid escalation of conflict. Vengeance and fault-finding.	Attempts to confront and resolve issues.	Defines issues. Uses problem solving, decision making, compromise, and conflict-containment skills.
CONTROL/ JEALOUSY	Monitors phone and friends. Sexualizes. Fixated on real or imagined infidelity.	Recognizes balance in separate and together interests. Individuates.	Supports spouse's independence. Secure in relationship.
SEX ROLES/ MARITAL DEPENDENCY	Emphasizes issues of obedience, power, dominance, and submission. Believes in rigid traditional sex roles and authoritarian decision making. Threatened by spouse's competence.	Is somewhat flexible in duties and decision making.	Encourages spouse's competence and independence. Fluid sex roles. Democratic and egalitarian.
ISOLATION/ SOCIAL SUPPORT	Fears or is suspicious of others. Does not request help. No supportive friends, family, or outside activities.	Uses phone, visits, goes out with spouse. Asks for help during crises.	Interacts with friends. Reciprocates helping acts. Engages in independent activities.

TIME-OUT

It is not uncommon for couples to report that tension and verbal abuse increase during the early weeks of treatment. It may be that tension is raised and issues are touched on during this period that the couple is not fully prepared to deal with. As couples continue with treatment, they acquire the skills to control their anger and contain the level of interpersonal conflict; however, at first it is essential that a time-out procedure be in place and available to interrupt the violence cycle. To establish a time-out procedure, a couple must do the following:

1. Identify the cues that signal rising anger. Although couples who have a history of violent episodes often progress very rapidly through the violence cycle, it is assumed that anger increases progressively rather than appearing full blown. The husband and wife should be assisted to become aware of the cues that accompany their own and their partner's rising anger. These cues can become part of an early warning system that signals that corrective action needs to be taken.

These cues can include:

- Physiological changes (rapid breathing, increased pulse rate, muscular contractions);
- Cognitive processes (Self-statements such as those involving labeling—"That bitch," catastrophizing—"I can't stand it," mind-reading—"She's doing it on purpose," vengeance—"I'll show her"); and
- Specific behaviors (pacing, shouting, pointing, clenching fists).

2. Identify "triggers" for physical violence. Triggers are behaviors that tend to escalate the level of anger during a confrontation and have been identified as immediately preceding violent outbursts in previous violent episodes. Often these triggers can be thought of as "clubs" that the couple will pick up when angry. Unresolved issues from the past, accusations, threats, and personal attacks are all examples of verbal triggers. Behavioral triggers often include acts that may symbolize disdain or abandonment such as attempting to leave the home, destroying possessions, or taking off wedding rings etc.

3. Establish the time-out signal. The couple should next agree on a signal that either partner can use to indicate concern about the level of anger. The signal should be neutral and nonblaming. Making a T signal with the hands or stating "time-out" in a neutral tone will both work. "I am getting angry" or "We are getting angry" is preferable to "You are getting angry" or "You are making me angry," which lead to defensiveness and counterattack rather than the desired response of temporary disengagement.

4. Decide where each spouse will go during time-out. Any location that will physically separate the couple will suffice as long as it has been agreed upon previously. In the absence of a clear prior agreement, there is the risk that leaving will be seen as abandonment and elicit efforts at restraint.

5. *Duration of time-out.* A time limit for time-outs should be agreed upon initially. If the signaling has been timely, even a relatively brief separation will serve to interrupt the violence sequence. However, the spouse who calls the time-out is responsible for signaling readiness to resume the discussion. It should be clearly understood that the discussion must always be resumed so that time-out does not become an avoidance tactic. Whether or not the time-out signal was used appropriately can be debated at this point, but not prior to the separation. It should be understood that time-out can be signaled again should either party be concerned again about escalation.

6. *Set rules to be followed during time-out.* The behavior that each party can and cannot engage in during time-out should be specified. Leaving the property, driving the car, going to a friend's, calling home, and drinking alcohol are all behaviors to consider when establishing the rules.

The Time-out Contract can be used by clients to establish a time-out procedure. In a group setting, clients should be encouraged to share and discuss their contracts. This permits the agreement to be refined, and making the commitment publicly has been found to increase compliance. The individual client who is still living with his spouse can take the Time-out Contract home and complete it with his wife. The film *Deck the Halls* (available from O.D.N. Productions, 74 Varick St., Room 304, New York, N.Y. 10013) can be used, if desired, to help clients identify the triggers and cues in a conflict situation.

It may also be useful at this time for clients to discuss contingency plans for protection in case of further violence. In these plans, the husband and wife list the protective action that they will take should violence occur again. A contingency contract is found in Chapter Nine. This form is usually completed by clients at the end of treatment as an additional prompt to remain violence free. But if the therapist feels that additional episodes of violence are likely, the contract can be included at any point in treatment.

EXERCISE 1

SELF-DESCRIPTION

Distribute the Self-Description Worksheet to clients. Explain that some of the words or descriptive phrases have been used in the past by clients to describe themselves. State that these are not permanent, God-given traits, but behaviors that clients may or may not have engaged in, which are certainly subject to change.

Ask them to check any that seem to some extent to fit them. If this exercise is being assigned for couples, ask them to work independently, filling out only their own description, then to share it with their spouse.

When working with a group, results can be totaled and listed on the board as a group profile. Discuss what characteristics clients would like to work on most in order to change.

PROGRAM PRINCIPLES HANDOUT

1. The primary goal of the program is to eliminate violence in the home.

2. Although anger and conflict are normal elements of family life, violence has no place in the family and is never justified.

3. Abusiveness is a learned behavior.

4. Abusive behavior is a relationship issue, but it is ultimately the responsibility of the male to control physical violence.

5. Abusiveness is a desperate but ultimately maladaptive effort to effect relationship change.

6. Abusiveness tends to escalate in severity and frequency if not treated.

CLIENT'S CONTRACT

I understand the goals of this program and agree to participate fully. I am aware that the main purpose is to eliminate threats and physical violence in my home. To this end, I will accept responsibility for identifying those factors that have contributed to past violent behavior and for learning new skills to deal with anger, frustration, and conflict.

To successfully complete the program, I will:

1. Not threaten or commit violence against any member of my family.
2. Attend and participate fully in each session.
3. Complete all assignments.
4. Respect the confidence of the group (if I am working in a group) by discussing sensitive issues only with other members of the program.
5. Contact a member of the staff immediately for assistance with any domestic conflict that escalates to a potentially dangerous level.

SIGNED _____

_____ Therapist

_____ Date

ATTITUDE SURVEY HANDOUT

It is perfectly natural as we begin for you to have mixed feelings. Take a look at your attitude and try to analyze and understand it, *not* change it. Please circle the number of any of the following that describe how you feel now:

1. *Resentment.* I don't like being told to do something, and I feel I don't need to be here.
2. *Skepticism.* I feel this won't help at all or could make things worse.
3. *Pride.* It's hard to think that my behavior is wrong or that I could have made things turn out better.
4. *Embarrassment.* The idea of talking about "private" business seems embarrassing.
5. *Hopelessness or Defeat.* I am convinced that nothing will help.
6. *Anger.* I am focusing on how I was mistreated before I got here.

Some assumptions or beliefs that will affect your attitude are:

"I am perfect."
"I may not be perfect, but whatever problems I did have are all under control now."
"It's my partner who needs help and needs to change."
"Our problems were caused by some outside force (alcohol, neighbors, police, etc.)."
"My partner has hurt me and now is going to pay."
"I can't control myself or change."
"My partner better change—or else."
"I've got things the way I want them and don't want any changes."

SELF-DESCRIPTION WORKSHEET

The following are ways that other clients have described themselves. Please go through this list and check those that seem to be most like you.

HUSBAND

_____ Blames others

_____ Impulsive

_____ Loses temper easily

_____ Will not apologize or back down

_____ Always tense and tight

_____ Can't leave work at work

_____ Competitive

_____ Does not praise or compliment

_____ Possessive

_____ Perfectionistic

_____ Attempts to control

_____ Puts down others

_____ Self-centered and demanding

_____ Inflexible

_____ Overreacts to annoyances

_____ Macho

_____ Trouble in expressing emotions

_____ Opinionated

_____ Trouble expressing ideas

_____ Drinks too much

WIFE

_____ Demanding

_____ Passive

_____ Isolated

_____ Few outside interests

_____ Angry

_____ Depressed

_____ Critical of others

_____ Trouble making decisions

_____ Dedicated to family

_____ Too involved with children

_____ Holds things inside

_____ Resentful

_____ Worn out

_____ Can't sleep

_____ Drinks too much

_____ Accepts too much blame

_____ Picks and complains

_____ Lacks confidence

_____ Clings to family

_____ Feels confused and "crazy"

TIME-OUT CONTRACT

1. The cues that _____ is getting angry are _____

Husband

   _____

   _____

   _____

   The cues that _____ is getting angry are _____

Wife

   _____

   _____

   _____

2. The triggers we need to avoid are _____

   _____

   _____

   _____

3. The neutral, nonblaming time-out signal we will use is _____

   _____

   _____

4. When either of us gives this signal,

   _____ will go _____

Husband

   _____ will go _____

Wife

5. The time-out period will last _____

   At the end of this time we will _____

6. During the time-out we will observe the following rules _____

   _____

   _____

   _____

SIGNED _____   _____

        Husband   Wife

_____ Date _____

        Therapist

Chapter Three

Understanding Violence

Abusive couples need to understand the pattern of their violent behavior in order to change this behavior. The cycle of violence in abusive incidents is examined in this chapter. The influence of violence in childhood on clients is also explored.

Violence is rarely an isolated event in the life of a relationship. Although even a single isolated violent episode, when it does occur, can have lasting implications in terms of upsetting the balance of power and trust in a relationship, the much more common pattern is for violence to recur with increasing frequency and seriousness. Not only do couples tend to resort to violence more frequently once the first episode occurs, but conflict tends to escalate much more rapidly in the course of any given argument. For these reasons, it is important for couples to recognize that violence is not an isolated, random event. Rather, there is a sequence or pattern to violence that couples can learn to recognize and use to predict and control the occurrence of subsequent violent episodes. The key to this process is to understand the sequence and recognize the signs of escalating violence so that they become signals for taking appropriate conflict containment steps.

Data from the Straus et al. survey (1981) support the view that violence in the American family is both a high frequency and a recurring phenomenon. The survey found that 3.8 percent of wives, or about 1 out of every 26 American wives, are beaten by their husbands in any given year. The term "beaten" does not refer to pushing, grabbing, or shoving. The 3.8 percent figure refers to incidents of severe violence with husbands attacking their wives by kicking, biting, or punching; hitting with some object; or threatening to use, or actually using, a knife or gun on them. The statistics for husband beating by wives in this survey were even higher, again supporting the view that violence is not an issue just for males but, instead, is a behavior engaged in by both sexes. About 4.6 percent of the women surveyed, or 1 out of every 22 wives, engaged in one of the above acts.

The Straus et al. data substantiated both the fact that there is an extraordinarily high level of severe violence in the American family,

59

and also that when such violence does occur it tends to be repeated. Violent abuse was repeated three or more times during the year by 47 percent of husbands who beat their wives and 53 percent of wives who beat their husbands. Violence was not repeated during the year in only one-third of the families.

Our observations on the frequency and evolution of the pattern of violence between spouses were suggested in the description of expressive and instrumental violence in Chapter One. We have observed that acts of expressive violence are engaged in somewhat more frequently by women than men and that over time violent behaviors become more deliberate and instrumental. The most serious acts of deliberate violence, or battering, are typically inflicted by males on females. The tendency of violence to increase in frequency and severity and to become more resistive to treatment reinforces the importance of early intervention.

Serious violence is relatively uncommon prior to marriage. The most common pattern seems to be for anger and violence to be held in check during courtship and the early days of marriage only to emerge gradually. There are probably several factors that contribute to this phenomenon, one of which is the tendency to overlook differences prior to marriage. After marriage, however, behaviors previously considered tolerable idiosyncracies may take on an altogether different meaning because they must be put up with "forever."

Often the level of verbal aggression escalates first in a relationship. This may be followed by throwing things (Straus et al. [1981] found that women are six times as likely as men to throw objects), destroying possessions, making threatening gestures, and putting fists through walls.

At one time it was felt that "blowing off steam" through behaviors such as shouting and swearing would tend to drain off violent energy and, thus, reduce the likelihood of physical violence. Psychoanalytical theorists have talked as if there were a fixed amount of aggressive energy in the body, as though human beings constituted a closed energy system—but people are not teapots. It is important for clients to realize that it is now well substantiated in the literature that rather than having a cathartic or beneficial effect, giving free rein to expressions of anger actually increases the likelihood of physical violence. Fuming and complaining tend to legitimize rage and increase anger through rehearsal (Tavris, 1982), and couples who engage in violent verbal arguments are much more likely to escalate their arguments to physical violence (Bandura & Walters, 1963).

The response of the other party to these early violent outbursts may play an important role in perpetuating the pattern. The wife may join in the escalating violence, or she may engage in some behaviors that communicate tacit acceptance of the violence. Either of these responses contributes to the likelihood of an increasing level of violent expression. Frequently, the wife will participate in the process by assuming that the violence is, in some way, her fault. She convinces herself of the validity of her husband's accusations, thereby assuming responsibility for this behavior. This distorted perception is reinforced since it enables the wife to experience some control in a situation where she would otherwise feel helpless and without control. If it is her fault, then she can make sure the violence will not recur by changing her behavior. She may deny both her own anger and the seriousness of the situation. External factors such as alcohol or work-related pressures are often viewed as the causes of the violence in her efforts to deny the existence of a more profound problem. She may further participate in, and indeed become an accomplice to, the violence by concealing its occurrence from others and helping her husband avoid facing the consequences of his violent behavior. It should be noted that the same maintaining behaviors are frequently engaged in by husbands when the wife initiates the violence.

THE THREE-PHASE VIOLENCE CYCLE

Lenore Walker (1979) has identified a three-phase violence cycle. The phases are:

1. The tension-building phase;
2. The explosion or acute violent episode;
3. The remorse phase.

Her formulations have evidently been based on observations of battering relationships (instrumental violence). Our work has been mainly with couples whose violent behavior can be thought of as the product of the escalation of violence in the context of an argument (expressive violence).

Walker's violence cycle model, although derived from observations of battering relationships, also has applications for work with couples involved in a recurring pattern of escalating conflict. The three phases may not be as pronounced in nonbattering relationships; however, they do provide a conceptual framework for couples to apply in understanding their own violent behavior.

Phase One—Tension Building

This is a period of mounting stress and tension. Usually, the stressors (such as worry over finances or conflict over in-laws) are not put into words, but are held inside where they tend to be compounded and magnified. Cooperation turns to faultfinding which is focused on the relationship. Communication and the exchange of caring behaviors, which may characterize the relationship at its best, diminish as the husband and wife tend to sullenly withdraw from each other. Frequently they will begin to make themselves angry by collecting injustices. They are likely to become critical, focusing on problems and actively looking for evidence to justify and magnify anger. They may attempt to pick a fight or confront each other. Being aware of the cues of their rising anger (physiological changes, cognitive processes, and specific behaviors) can make clients aware that corrective action is needed at this point.

Either partner may respond to the rising tension by becoming increasingly apprehensive and may withdraw, lash back, or become quite attentive and subservient. It is not uncommon for couples who have experienced the cycle a number of times to develop a sense that violence is coming and that it is inevitable. At this point, the husband may get drunk, anticipating a violent confrontation, or the wife may provoke the violence in order to bring the tension and dread to an end. Phase One may last anywhere from an hour to several months.

Phase Two—The Acute Violent Episode

Typically, Phase One leads to an abusive episode in which the mounting tension is explosively discharged. Immediately prior to the violence, there is often the feeling that a point of inevitability has been reached. Both parties are likely to feel victimized and out of control.

It is important for couples to be aware of triggers that symbolize disdain or abandonment, which are often used to elicit violence at this stage. The trigger may be verbal or physical behavior such as returning home intoxicated, throwing the spouse's clothes outside, threatening to leave, destroying a prized possession, or intruding into the spouse's personal space.

A common occurrence just before the violence is for one party, usually the man, to withdraw by refusing to communicate further. In many cases, husbands report that they cannot keep up with their wives, who seem to think and speak faster and generally seem to have the advantage in any verbal conflict. The retreat, then, is often out of frustration. The husband may signal that he fears he is about to "lose it" and demand that his wife "back off." She, in turn, experiences this withdrawal as a sign that he doesn't care or is not taking her concerns seriously, and this misunderstanding is likely to increase her efforts to break through to him by moving closer, speaking more loudly, or physically preventing him from leaving. The conflict escalates through this pattern of circular feedback as each partner misunderstands the intentions and behavior of the other.

There is some speculation that males, in the process of growing up, develop various signals for giving up in their play at fighting with other males that females might not understand. These signals terminate the fights before real violence and injury occur. Females, who typically have not been socialized in this manner, may not develop the ability to detect or recognize the significance of these signals. It is not uncommon for a man to report that he had tried to signal his spouse of the impending danger before abusive incidents and that the spouse had seemed to disregard the warning.

Another factor related to the acculturation of males that may occur at this stage (especially in a subculture of violence) that may not be understood by women is a norm that demands a physical response from a man to preserve his dignity when faced with certain derogatory remarks. This norm may leave both parties feeling victimized.

The value of making these signaling systems and norms explicit and in generally recognizing the role of triggers in the violence cycle is apparent. The earlier in the violence cycle that couples become aware of the escalation process and make an effort to avert violence, the more effective they will be in achieving this goal. Couples who are not aware of the sequential steps in the escalation of the violence cycle and of the role of signals and triggers usually fail to realize that violence is imminent. By the time they recognize the potential for violence, it is often too late to avert the outcome.

Phase Three—Remorse

Immediately following the explosive release of the violent episode comes a period of relative calm. The tension that had been building during Phase One has been dissipated. The more violent partner may experience remorse, which is expressed in the form of efforts to gain forgiveness. Apologies, statements that it will never happen again, expressions of physical affection, and gifts are common. This behavior is prompted by a genuine sense of guilt and also by fear of losing the spouse by having gone too far. The remorse experienced during this phase may make an accurate evaluation of the situation difficult and serve to perpetuate the cycle of violence.

The level of intimacy in this phase may exceed what the husband and wife experience at any other time. They may be able to disclose feelings of weakness and vulnerability that generally remain well concealed. There may be a shift in power in which the wife feels protective and as if she is the stronger of the two. This shift in power is consistent with the principle that in any relationship the person with the least to lose has the most power. In the abusive situation, the person who has been physically abused and may threaten to leave the relationship has suddenly shifted from being powerless to powerful. She may try to punish her husband or get expressions of contrition from him which, although satisfying in the short run, only set the stage for further power struggles once the husband again feels secure in the permanence of the relationship.

When intervention occurs several hours after the episode, both parties may be well into Phase Three. In their mutual feelings of closeness and protectiveness, they may be secure in the belief that the problem has been solved and violence will not occur again. Consequently, they may resist any form of assistance. It is this ray-of-hope phenomenon and the belief that "love is enough" that contribute to the resistance to intervention.

June Wiest, in a thoughtful article on the treatment of violent individuals (Wiest, 1981), has identified several stages of remorse. Although her observations are based on work at a state hospital for the criminally insane, the concept of remorse as she develops it is quite applicable to domestic violence. The first stage that she describes is that of the confession where the offender is likely to say, "Yes, I did it." The second stage is the acceptance of punishment or the acceptance of treatment as substitute for punishment. At this stage the person seems motivated when he states, "What I did was wrong and I deserve this punishment (or treatment)." Wiest refers to the third stage as denial. Here the person ceases to complain or attempt to undo and begins to grieve. The grief, however, is primarily for himself—for the inconvenience, the shame, and for the adverse consequences of the violent episode. The final stage is remorse, which is experienced as grief for the victim. It requires the ability to empathize with the plight of the victim. The level of remorse experienced by clients, although initially obscured by defensiveness, is an excellent indication of motivation and the prognosis for positive change.

Exercise 2, The Violence Cycle, uses the Violence Cycle Worksheet to help couples recognize the pattern in their own episodes of violence in part A and includes an optional exercise for analyzing the violence cycle in the film *Deck the Halls* in part B.

VIOLENCE AND ANGER IN CHILDHOOD

Abusive individuals are likely to have experienced or witnessed violence as children. The extent to which adults recreate the violence of their childhood has been well documented in the work of Straus et al. (1981). In a national survey, they discovered that men and women who had seen their parents engage in physical violence were almost 3 times as likely to hit their own wives or husbands as those who had not witnessed comparable parental violence. Men who grew up with very violent parents had a rate of wife beating 10 times greater than that of men who were raised in nonviolent homes. Women raised by very violent parents had a husband-beating rate 6 times higher than daughters of nonviolent parents. Clearly, witnessing violence during childhood makes it more likely that people will tend to be violent in their own marriages. The more serious the witnessed violence, the stronger the tendency to be violent as an adult, and the quicker the escalation from expressive to instrumental violence.

Additionally, survey results also indicate that those people who received a high level of physical punishment as teenagers are 4 times as likely to beat their spouses as those who were not physically punished. The trend is strongest for daughters who were punished by their mothers and sons who were punished by their fathers. It appears that people tend to model most strongly the violent behavior of the same-sex parent.

It is data such as these that establish the influence of childhood experiences on subsequent adult violent behavior. Each generation seems to learn to be violent by having been members of violent families as children; thus, violence begets violence. The learning may take several forms:

1. Children who see their parents hit each other grow up to *model* this behavior in their own marriages.
2. The more children are hit by their parents, the more inclined they are to grow up to use hitting as a tool for influencing and controlling others.

The treatment implications are clear. Clients must learn to:

1. Recognize the influence of past learning experiences on their current behavior;
2. Acknowledge that if they were subjected to significant levels of violence as children they are at risk to continue this pattern;

3. Attempt to understand the influence of the values and behavior experienced as children so that they can exercise an
   increased level of choice over whether the influence will continue; and
4. Recognize the impact that their behavior is likely to have on
   their own children.

It is also important for clients to realize that, although certain
childhood experiences may increase the likelihood of their acting in a
similar manner as adults, these past experiences do not inevitably
cause or dictate the behavior. Experiencing or witnessing violence
may predispose a person to violence, but many people who had similar
experiences have chosen not to be violent and learned how to behave
otherwise. It should be emphasized that these experiences may continue to exert an influence if they are not acknowledged, examined,
and then deliberately rejected.

Some of the lessons (Straus et al., 1981) that early exposure to
violence and physical punishment may communicate include:

1. Those who love you are likely to be those who hit you. If the
   lesson is incorporated as a child, it can take the form of those
   you love are those you hit as an adult. The fact that parents
   use physical punishment such as slapping a child who is
   reaching for fire teaches not only that fire is dangerous, but
   also that slapping is an appropriate means of influencing
   those you love.
2. If violence is used to effect a desirable end, such as helping a
   child avoid injury, it is morally right. The ends can be used
   to justify the means.
3. Violence is permissible when other means have failed. The
   number of times people say, "I've tried everything, and
   spanking is the only thing that works" attests to the popu-
   larity of this lesson.

There is evidence that severe punishment administered for being
aggressive markedly increases the level of aggression, particularly in
the case of boys (Sears, Maccoby, & Levin, 1957). It is interesting to
consider the mixed messages a child is subjected to when he is physically punished for being physically aggressive.

The Anger Lessons Worksheet promotes discussion of these issues as well as the related issues of sex role stereotypes and the sense of
fear and insecurity that accompanies violence both in childhood and
adulthood. Often, clients who are reluctant to discuss their attitudes

toward the current violence in their marriages are able to convey their feelings through discussing the violence they experienced as children. This worksheet can serve as an introduction to the anger-control techniques in the next chapter.

The Anger Log I is also assigned as homework. During the first few weeks it is used to capture incidents of anger and violence for analysis. Clients record the incident or event in which they experienced anger, the date and time of the incident, the degree of anger as estimated on a 0–100 scale (100 equals maximum rage), the thoughts that occur during and just after the incident, and finally, the outcome.

EXERCISE 2

THE VIOLENCE CYCLE

A. Distribute copies of the Violence Cycle Worksheet and ask each couple to fill one out for their last violent episode. Stressors, cues, triggers, and evidence of remorse should be detailed. Discuss the worksheets during the session.

B. (Optional) Show the O.D.N. film *Deck the Halls* available from O.D.N. Productions, 74 Varick St., Room 304, New York, NY 10013. This excellent portrayal of a violent episode in the life of a family lends itself to being analyzed in the terms of the violence cycle. After viewing the film, have couples fill out the Violence Cycle Worksheet, identifying the stressors evident during the tension building phase, the cues of rising anger, the triggers for the violent episode, and finally the manifestations of remorse. Use the worksheets as the basis for discussion of the cycle of violence. Often, asking the question "Who caused the violence?" or "Whose fault was it?" elicits a debate which can be used to introduce the circular model of causation.

VIOLENCE CYCLE WORKSHEET

PHASE ONE—TENSION BUILDING

Stressors: _____

_____

_____

_____

Cues: _____

_____

_____

_____

PHASE TWO—VIOLENT EPISODE

Triggers: _____

_____

_____

_____

PHASE THREE—REMORSE

Evidence of Remorse: _____

_____

_____

_____

ANGER LESSONS WORKSHEET

1. How did your father act when he was angry? _____
   _____
   _____
   _____

2. How did your mother act when she was angry? _____
   _____
   _____
   _____

3. How did they handle conflict? _____
   _____
   _____
   _____

4. Was anybody afraid at home? _____
   _____
   _____
   _____

5. What did you learn at home about:
   How men are angry? _____
   _____
   _____
   _____

   How women are angry? _____
   _____
   _____
   _____

ANGER LESSONS WORKSHEET (cont.)

Resolving conflict? _____

_____

_____

_____

6. How did you express anger as a child? _____

_____

_____

_____

7. What did you learn that you would like to change? _____

_____

_____

_____

_____

ANGER LOG I

DATE/ TIME	INCIDENT	ANGER LEVEL (0–100)	THOUGHTS DURING AND AFTER THE INCIDENT	OUTCOME

Chapter Four

Anger Control

How anger is conceptualized, expressed, and controlled is at the core of treatment for those involved in domestic violence. People who have engaged in spouse abuse typically have a difficult time articulating their emotions, tend to hold things inside, and tend to experience or label any state of emotional arousal as anger.

When clients state that someone or some event "made" them angry, it is not a conscious attempt to avoid responsibility, but an accurate reflection of their own experience. In their minds, they are victims provoked into destructive outbursts for which they later may feel some degree of remorse and embarrassment. They rarely believe that they have any influence over their emotional state and feel only tenuous control over how their emotions will find expression in behavior. They are also often deficient in assertive interpersonal skills (Rosenbaum & O'Leary, 1981) and alternate between efforts at holding in their anger and expressing anger in the form of poorly controlled, aggressive outbursts. They will frequently withdraw and suppress the expression of any negative feelings. This leads to a period of increased tension which may result in an aggressive outburst. Following the outburst, the individual may feel apologetic and in order to atone will put up with negative conduct on the part of the other until the tension leads to another outburst.

Anger control is developed through recognizing how beliefs, values, and cognitions create anger. The choice in responding to a potentially anger-arousing event is then expanded beyond either holding it in or expressing it in a hostile, pressured form, to choosing not to get angry in the first place or at least not getting extremely angry.

"Man is not disturbed by events, but by the view he takes of them." This frequently quoted statement by the Stoic philosopher Epictetus is the basis for this book's approach to anger control, which is founded on the Rational-Emotive Therapy of Albert Ellis (1962) and the cognitive approach of Aaron Beck (1979) and David Burns (1980).

This view of anger control can be introduced to clients with these statements: "There is only one person on the face of this earth who can make you angry, and that is you. Even if your spouse wanted to make you mad, she could not, as you would *always* have a choice. Regardless of how unjust, outrageous, or provocative her behavior, she did not, cannot, and will not make you angry. Only you can make yourself angry."

The typical reaction to these statements is one of disbelief. It is only after hearing several presentations of the anger-control model, working with the anger log, and reviewing numerous examples that clients can begin to view themselves as having control over their anger. When they later begin to report successful experiences in anger control, these reports are accompanied by a profound sense of mastery and optimism, as a way out of the cycle of violence then has been recognized.

A detailed discussion of the theoretical foundations of this approach to anger control, examples of the types of cognitive processes, values, and beliefs that contribute to anger, and strategies for combating them follow.

THE A-B-C THEORY OF EMOTIONAL AROUSAL

Spouse abusers generally believe that emotions are basic, primary qualities of human life over which little or no control can be exercised. Averill's (1974) description of emotions as "passions" by which people are "gripped," "seized," or "torn" is not far from the view of those who have participated in serious abusive incidents. They tend to believe that emotions are irrational, noncognitive components of their lives, outside of the realm of personal control.

It requires considerable effort for them to begin to understand that thinking and emotions are not two separate processes, but that at a practical level, they are the same thing. Emotions do not have an independent existence in that they cannot be automatically elicited, other than for very brief periods of time, without first perceiving and then interpreting and continuing to think about an incident. It is not then the event itself, but the interpretation of that event, mediated by certain cognitive processes, that results in the emotion. According to Ellis (1962), what we refer to as emotion is usually excited, passionate, and strong evaluation of some person or event. There is no such thing as an "anger reflex" similar to jerking our knees when they are tapped. All anger is preceded by thought processes in which the event is perceived, interpreted, and then acted upon.

Ellis has described this approach as the A-B-C theory of emotional arousal. A stands for the incident or activating event, B for the individual's perceptions or beliefs about the event, and C for the consequent emotion. We are predisposed to thinking of A causing C, that is, of the activating event leading directly to the consequent emotion. However, the important intervening step over which we can exert considerable influence is B, our perception, definition, and belief about the event. Ellis has described step B as "self-talk": the internal thought processes we are constantly engaged in during our conscious lives, the sentences with which we define and interpret the world.

When our self-talk is accurate and rational, we function well, but, when the self-talk becomes irrational and highly charged, we experience disruptive, maladaptive emotional states. To return to the A-B-C model, it is irrational self-talk at step B that creates emotions, not the events themselves. For example:

A. Antecedent event: Jim returns home from work to discover that his wife has not cleaned up the house as he had requested.
B. Belief or self-talk: "She never does what I ask her. If she loved me she would have done it. It's not fair. I work all day and she just sits around. I can't stand it!"
C. Consequent emotions: anger and resentment.

In this case, Jim would be likely to report that A caused C, that the sight of the untidy house automatically elicited feelings of resentment and anger.

Exercise 3, Turning It Upside Down, helps counter the resistance that clients sometimes have to the idea that they, and not other people or events, make themselves angry. Exercise 4, Attribution, demonstrates that it is the meaning we assign to an event rather than the event itself that determines our emotional response.

COGNITIVE DISTORTIONS AND IRRATIONAL BELIEFS

David Burns (1980) has referred to the self-talk process as "automatic thoughts" because these thoughts often occur without intention or awareness. He has identified several types of automatic thoughts, or cognitive distortions, that frequently accompany anger. These are:

1. Labeling. Labeling involves categorizing someone in a totally negative manner. Rather than thinking of people as personalities comprised of complex mixtures of both positive and negative qualities, we reduce them to objects bearing a single label. The focus shifts from undesirable behavior to total personality. We think of people as jerks, idiots, shit-heads—all emotionally charged overgeneralizations. We often categorize someone as totally bad or totally worthless to protect our own self-esteem; if we feel threatened, rejected, or disagreed with, we may engage in labeling to disqualify the opponent.

2. *Mind-reading.* When we assume to know the reason why a person acted in a certain way, we are mind-reading. We attribute motives to people that explain their actions to our satisfaction. Rarely do we bother to check out our assumptions, acting instead as if they were inevitably true. It is the assumption of another's deliberate, malevolent intent that fuels anger and the desire for revenge. These assumptions tend to become self-fulfilling prophecies because if people do act in ways that are inconsistent with our negative assumptions, we fail to recognize it and reward them. An example of this type of thinking is "If she loved me she would have cleaned up the house. Since she no longer loves me, I will punish and reject her."

3. *Fortune-telling.* Mind-reading is often linked to fortune-telling or predicting the future. We may decide that because an event has occurred in the past it will continue forever. For example: "She will never change" or "Even if I changed, she wouldn't; therefore, it would never work."

4. *Magnification.* Magnification, or catastrophizing, involves exaggerating the importance or consequences of a negative event. It is difficult to become very angry over an event that we think of as inconvenient or merely annoying. "It's horrible," "I can't stand it," "She's driving me crazy" are all exaggerations that serve to heighten emotional arousal. Obviously if someone is still around to talk about it, he can stand it, and it's not driving him crazy.

5. *Should statements.* Should statements are cognitive distortions that result in feelings of anger and frustration. We translate preferences ("I would very much like it to be this way") into commands or demands ("Because I would very much like it, it *should* be"). Ellis has referred to this process as "musterbation" and has employed the injunction "stop shoulding on yourself" to remind people of this common practice.

Should statements imply that we are *entitled* to pleasure and satisfaction and that it's not fair if we don't get them. This moralistic and judgmental attitude is the basis for most anger. By expressing our preferences in the form of moralistic absolutes, we experience a sense of being victimized when our desires go unmet. The sense of injustice, the related emotions of self-righteous anger, and the desire to punish or set things right sustain anger and fuel interpersonal conflict.

Should statements, then, involve the implicit expression of pre-ferences as inflexible rules about how we and others should act. The rules represent "fairness" from *our* perspective and are not subject to debate. A violation of the rules results in judging, finding fault, and casting blame. By insisting that others should know our rules and comply with them, we are doomed to continual disappointment, frustration, and anger.

Ellis (1977) has listed the following four irrational beliefs that contribute most to the experience of anger:

1. "How *awful* or *terrible* that you treat me like this!"
2. "I *can't stand* your unfair behavior!"
3. "You *should not* act in that unacceptable manner toward me!" "You *must* treat me fairly."
4. "Because of your unacceptable behavior, you deserve punishment and are a *rotten person!*"

These four beliefs generate anger and tend to personalize the conflict, shifting the focus from the original conflict issue to blaming the individual. The steps have been summarized by Ellis with the following colorful, and easily remembered, terms:

Awfulizing
Cant't-stand-it-itus
Shoulding and musting
Undeservingness or damnation

Identifying Automatic Thoughts

Once participants have been exposed to the theory of anger arousal, and to examples of the cognitive distortions and irrational beliefs that generate anger, they are ready to begin to learn anger-control techniques. Incidents of anger written by clients on the Anger Log I are analyzed to teach these control techniques. The following information can often be determined by discussing the anger log:

1. Date and time. Occasionally patterns emerge that suggest that certain times or days represent high-risk times for anger. For some, the early morning hours or weekends may be identified as times when conflict should be avoided or adaptive coping strategies employed (i.e., a search for positive activities on a Sunday afternoon if this is a high-risk time).

2. Incident. Clients can learn to distinguish between actual events and interpretations of those events by describing the anger-arousing incident as objectively as possible. Having them describe the event briefly and in just those terms that would be captured by a TV camera if the event were being recorded helps them make this distinction.

3. Level of anger. By applying a value from 0 to 100, with 100 representing absolute maximum rage, the amount of anger experienced can be quantified. The values are useful in determining the relative anger aroused by different situations and for measuring the effectiveness of subsequent intervention strategies.

4. Outcome. The outcome together with the level of anger constitutes step C in the A-B-C model of emotional arousal. In analyzing the anger log, it is helpful to initially skip step B, the thoughts about the event, to reinforce the idea that we usually erroneously think of A causing C. Having clients first describe the incident and their feelings when explaining and reviewing entries from their anger logs reflects the way they experience the situation.

When they return to step B, and consider the beliefs or internal sentences surrounding the event, they are able to acknowledge that indeed this step may have preceded the emotional arousal. Analysis of outcome can often be used to determine the degree of control being exercised and also the amount of any secondary gains (events that occur as a result of the expression of anger that may serve to reinforce it). "I punched him in the nose and felt great," "I shook my fist and my wife gave in," or "I felt so upset that I went out and got drunk" suggest outcomes that may be rewarding the expression of anger.

5. Thoughts during and after the incident. Initially these automatic thoughts give clients the most difficulty because clients need to practice monitoring thought processes and thinking of them in the form of internal sentences or thoughts that can be recorded. Descriptions of the most common cognitive distortions and irrational beliefs will facilitate this process as will discussions of the automatic thoughts that may have been involved in each incident. When clients can identify their own automatic thoughts, mastery of the Anger Log I procedure has been demonstrated.

Refuting Automatic Thoughts

After working with and thoroughly discussing the Anger Log I for about 2 weeks, clients are usually able to readily identify their automatic anger-generating thoughts. The anger logs usually reflect a rather dramatic reduction in the frequency and intensity of angry thoughts and clients report a sense of confidence that they can, in fact, control the experience of anger and its expression. It is obvious that recognizing how anger is self-induced through the use of automatic thoughts is in itself a powerful tool for self-control.

When the clients are ready, the use of the Anger Log II is introduced and the focus is shifted from detecting automatic thoughts to actively refuting them. This technique is based upon those of Beck (1979) and Burns (1980) for logging and refuting emotions. Two additional steps are required to complete the Anger Log II as columns are included for recording rational thoughts and the subsequent level of anger experienced. The basic principle at this point is to substitute "cool" thoughts for "hot" ones, thereby reducing the level of anger-inducing self-talk. For example:

> INCIDENT: Wife late picking me up from work
> ANGER LEVEL: 90
> AUTOMATIC THOUGHTS (Hot): That jerk. She's always late. She's probably doing it on purpose. I can't stand it. I'd like to punch her in the nose.
> RATIONAL THOUGHTS (Cool): She's not always late, but she has been late several times in the past 2 weeks. It's an inconvenience and I don't like it, but I can stand it. Punching her in the nose would just make things worse, but I should let her know how I feel.

Again, considerable time is spent working with examples from the clients' anger logs. The most common anger-arousing cognitive distortions are listed here with suggestions for how clients can refute them (Burns, 1980).

1. Labeling. Describing the behavior, not the personality, of an individual is a way that clients can avoid labeling. They should be specific, avoid overgeneralizing, and use the person's name to avoid reducing him to an object. They can ask themselves if the label is totally accurate and always fits, or if it is only true for the moment. For example, instead of thinking "He's a jerk," they could think, "I don't like Jon's whining and complaining."

2. Mind-reading. Clients can be reminded to follow the principle of behavioral essence—"You are what you do." They should focus on behavior and avoid speculations about motives or intentions. Inferences about motives are always speculative; therefore, there is the possibility of error. Assumptions should be verified and held in check until confirmed. For example, instead of thinking "She's doing this to hurt me," clients could think, "I can't read her mind, so I really don't know why she's acting this way."

3. Fortune-telling. Predictions are only guesses about the future. Clients should be aware of the self-fulfilling prophecy "If you are convinced that things will not change for the better, they probably won't." Instead of thinking "My life will never get better," clients could think, "If I work at it, my life may become more pleasant."

4. Magnification. Quantifying statements by indicating precisely how often something happens, how undesirable it is, and so on is a way to fight magnification. Terms such as *always, never, everybody,* and *nobody* should be avoided. Clients should remember to look for exceptions. Instead of thinking "I can't stand the way she acts," clients could think, "It's an inconvenience, but it's not the end of the world" or "I don't like it but I can stand it."

5. Should statements. Clients can rewrite their rules that use should, ought, or must to have more flexible standards for themselves and others. They can challenge should statements by thinking of at least three exceptions and considering reasons why other people "should" have done exactly what they did. Writing the rules for the entire world and demanding perfection from others and self is exhausting and not particularly rewarding work. We are all fallible, more or less screwed-up human beings. Clients should try not to translate preferences into demands. For example, instead of thinking "She should not treat me this way," they could think "It would be nice if she didn't treat me this way" or "She's treated me this way before, so it's logical that she would continue to act this way."

The point is not to suggest that people should think in any one way but rather that they have a choice, and that the level of rhetoric or self-talk they employ influences the emotions experienced.

Exercise 5, Hot Words, demonstrates the effect of words and images on our emotions. The A-B-Cs of Anger Control Self-analysis Worksheet is given to clients as homework to build understanding of this anger-control technique.

The Anger Log II at the end of this chapter is usually introduced to clients after they have mastered identifying irrational thoughts on the Anger Log I and are ready to refute them.

ADVANTAGES AND DISADVANTAGES OF ANGER

"The perception of unfairness or injustice is the ultimate cause of most, if not all, anger. In fact, we could define anger as the emotion that corresponds in a one-to-one manner to your belief that you are being treated unfairly" (Burns, 1980, p. 145). This statement suggests why anger can be such a difficult emotion to work with. There is often a sense of satisfaction and moral superiority that accompanies the determination of unfairness which underlies anger. To view ourselves as being victimized entitles us to feel angry and to seek revenge; and, to equate our own personal desires with a fundamental rightness is to clothe them in terms of self-righteous morality. It's not simply that people are not doing what we would like of them, it is that they are betraying a basic code of fairness.

Anger is often experienced when our attempts to reach some goal are thwarted. It is anger that enables us to maintain the illusion that we are not giving in, but are continuing to fight for our own self-interest and are still in control. As long as we continue to stay angry, we can feel that we have not passively accepted defeat. In this sense, to abandon anger may be experienced as abandoning hope or as giving up. The problem is that anger and blame often contribute to a false sense of doing something about the original injustice. Blaming defends us against feelings of impotence but distracts from real goal attainment. Anxiety and vulnerability are masked by the arousal of anger. The suggestion to cease anger and blaming may be confused with the suggestion to give up.

Novaco (1976) has pointed out several additional positive coping functions associated with anger arousal that serve to make anger reinforcing and, therefore, hard to give up. Anger can energize behavior and allow more vigorous responses. It can have a communicative function. In relationships the expression of anger often signals the relative importance of the issue; problems may never be taken seriously until they are expressed in anger. Anger also induces a sense of potency and serves the self-promotional function of communicating the qualities of determination and expressiveness rather than anxiousness and apathy. Finally, the expression of anger and rage can be a remarkably effective way of influencing and controlling others. Anger is then reinforced by the deference and compliance of others.

The treatment issue is that of motivating clients to master and implement control strategies over an emotional state that:

1. Is often accompanied by a sense of moral righteousness;
2. Sustains a sense of control and mastery;
3. Masks anxiety and vulnerability; and
4. Is often reinforced by compliance in interpersonal situations.

Until clients have carefully considered both the short-term and the long-term consequences of their anger and determined that mastery of anger-control techniques are in their own best interest, motivation for change may be low. This consideration of long-term consequences can be strengthened in clients by asking them how long it would feel good if they were violent, what would happen afterwards, and what it would cost them.

The "Double Column Technique" (Burns, 1980) compares the advantages and disadvantages of anger in a situation to determine if continued anger is worthwhile. An example of the Double Column Technique follows.

Joe, a 23-year-old businessman, has been married 3 years. His wife, Alice, was employed when they were first married, but now stays home to care for their two young children. Joe has been feeling pressured by new responsibilities he has assumed at work and is frequently exhausted and irritable when he comes home in the evening. He has fallen into a pattern of criticizing Alice for the way the house looks and blaming her for their financial difficulties. The advantages and disadvantages of his anger are:

ADVANTAGES OF ANGER	DISADVANTAGES OF ANGER
1. It makes me feel good and self-righteous.	1. The good feeling doesn't last long.
2. I have the right to be angry because I work so hard.	2. I often feel guilty after blowing up.
3. It will show Alice that I won't be pushed around.	3. My anger makes her unhappy and we both end up more depressed.
4. It will make her sorry she has treated me badly.	4. My blame leads Alice to get defensive and then to get even.
5. It will make her shape up.	5. By focusing on her short-comings, she feels un-appreciated for what she does do.
6. I can justify not helping more around the house.	6. We often both stop try-ing and things get even worse.
7. I can get my way if Alice is afraid to upset me.	7. I really don't want a wife who is afraid of me. I would like for us to enjoy each other again.

ADVANTAGES OF ANGER	DISADVANTAGES OF ANGER
	8. The kids and neighbors are beginning to treat me like I'm a grouch.
	9. I will be more relaxed, predictable, and pleasant to be around if I control my anger.
	10. I will probably end up getting more of what I really want from Alice and from life.

Adaptation of (double column technique) "Advantages of Anger and Disadvantages of Anger" from *FEELING GOOD: The New Mood Therapy* by David D. Burns, M.D., Copyright © 1980 by David D. Burns, M.D.
Adapted by permission of William Morrow & Company

In this situation, the disadvantages of his anger outweighed the advantages, and Joe would probably have agreed to give up his anger. When long-term consequences are considered, the disadvantages of anger usually outweigh the advantages.

Exercise 6, The Double Column Technique, helps clients weigh the advantages and disadvantages of anger in their own situations.

EXERCISE 3

TURNING IT UPSIDE DOWN

Demonstrate personal control over emotional states by asking clients to imagine that they, for some reason, wish to become enraged. What steps could they follow to make themselves truly angry? By implication, if they can choose to make themselves angry, and follow certain procedures to achieve that end, they can also choose *not* to make themselves angry by avoiding those procedures. An additional point to be made with this exercise is that the amount of anger experienced is not determined by the severity of the event. They can make themselves terribly angry over a relatively trivial occurrence or, conversely, can choose to remain relatively untroubled by a severe event.

Ask clients to select an incident from their Anger Log I where the degree of anger was rated as fairly mild (under 30). If they don't have such an incident listed, they should think of one and record it on the log. Now, have them imagine that they had decided it was to their advantage to make themselves quite angry (over 90). Request that they list the thoughts that would enable them to achieve this goal.

EXERCISE 4

ATTRIBUTION

Ask clients to relax and imagine this scene: "You are waiting at work for your spouse to pick you up in the car. Forty-five minutes have gone by and your spouse has not yet arrived." Present the scene three times using the following interpretations, permitting enough time for clients to experience the associated emotions. Discuss the exercise following the final presentation.

1. "I hope the car hasn't broken down. Those tires weren't looking too good and it's getting dark. I hope she's all right."
2. "I wonder if there was some confusion. I think I said 5:00. Maybe she thought I meant to meet somewhere else."
3. "I'm stuck here at work and where is she? She's probably in some bar having a drink. Damn! I told her to be on time. I never can trust her."

EXERCISE 5

HOT WORDS

Lead clients through a brief deep-breathing exercise using the follow-ing script:

> Lean back in your chair and get as comfortable as possible. Allow your eyes to close slowly and try to let go of any worries, thoughts, or preoccupations you may have been carrying. Now slowly take a deep breath, hold it for a few seconds, then exhale slowly. As you exhale, try to relax and sink deeply into your chair. Imagine that each time you exhale, more and more tension is flowing from your body.

Then ask clients to engage in "bodyscanning," checking each part of the body to make sure they are fully relaxed, and to assign a value from 0–100 (100 is the most relaxed) to their present level of relaxa-tion. Now instruct them to say the following words to themselves subvocally, but with a great deal of conviction—"that asshole," "that shithead," "son-of-a-bitch," "I can't stand it," "I've got to have it"—and to notice the effect on their level of tension. Have them pay particular attention to which areas of the body respond, the location of muscular contractions, and other effects.

Ask clients to note their level of tension and then instruct them to substitute the following terms: "that misguided individual," "that fallible human being," "that complex person with negative and posi-tive qualities," "It's inconvenient, but I can stand it," "I would very much prefer it, but I don't absolutely need it." Have them check their level of tension and which areas of their body respond.

EXERCISE 6

DOUBLE COLUMN TECHNIQUE

Ask clients to consider a situation in which they experience consider-able anger and the urge to engage in blame and revenge. Subject the situation to a cost/benefit analysis by listing the advantages and the disadvantages. Both the short-term and long-term consequences should be included to determine if continuing with anger and blame is in the clients' self-interest.

THE A-B-Cs OF ANGER CONTROL
SELF-ANALYSIS WORKSHEET

In order to gain experience in applying the A-B-C model of anger control, complete the accompanying worksheet.

STEP 1—ACTIVATING EVENT OR INCIDENT

Write a brief, objective description of a recent incident in which you experienced anger. Write just the facts as they would have been recorded by a TV camera. List who, what, where, and when without elaboration or interpretation.

_____

_____

_____

_____

STEP 2—ANGER LEVEL

Assign a number to your anger level, 0 (none) to 100 (maximum).

_____

STEP 3—BEHAVIOR

Record what you *did* (the behavior engaged in) in response to the activating event (swore, left the room, clenched fist and jaws, etc.).

_____

_____

_____

_____

THE A-B-Cs OF ANGER CONTROL
SELF-ANALYSIS WORKSHEET (cont.)

STEP 4—AUTOMATIC THOUGHTS AND BELIEFS

Write down the internal sentences you were saying during or after the activating event. The more of these thoughts you can become aware of, the better, so write down several. (Examples: "I can't stand it." "It's not fair." "I'd like to . . .")

_____

_____

_____

_____

STEP 5— SELF-ANALYSIS QUESTIONS

Answer each of the following questions either yes or no to analyze whether or not your automatic thoughts increase your level of anger and discomfort.

	YES	NO
● Are my automatic thoughts based on an objective, rational interpretation of the event?	____	____
● Does my anger help me achieve my long-term goals or is it simply disruptive?	____	____
● Am I angry at someone who truly meant to hurt me?	____	____
● Do my automatic thoughts contribute to a positive attitude and sense of well-being?	____	____

If you answered yes to all four questions, your anger is probably adaptive and within acceptable limits. Congratulations, you can stop at this point.

If you answered no to any of the four questions, your anger is probably maladaptive and excessive, and you will find it helpful to complete the rest of the exercise.

THE A-B-Cs OF ANGER CONTROL
SELF-ANALYSIS WORKSHEET (cont.)

STEP 6—RATIONAL THOUGHTS

Substitute rational thoughts for any automatic thoughts listed for Step 3 that increase your anger and discomfort.

_____

_____

_____

_____

STEP 7—FINAL ANGER LEVEL

Assign a number (0–100) to your anger after substituting rational thoughts for automatic thoughts. The greater the difference between the values listed in Step 2 and Step 7, the more successful you have been in refuting your irrational, anger-producing thoughts.

_____

_____

STEP 8—RATIONAL BEHAVIOR

List the rational behavior you intend to engage in now or for similar activating events in the future.

_____

_____

_____

_____

ANGER LOG II

DATE/ TIME	INCIDENT	ANGER LEVEL (0-100)	AUTOMATIC THOUGHTS (Hot)	RATIONAL THOUGHTS (Cool)	OUTCOME	ANGER LEVEL (0-100)

Chapter Five

Additional Anger-Control Techniques

Although the anger-control technique of identifying and actively refuting the values, attitudes, and beliefs that led to the experience of anger in the first place constitutes the primary anger-control technique employed throughout the program, there are a number of supplemental techniques that can be introduced when appropriate. These additional techniques should only be employed after clients have become thoroughly familiar with the A-B-C theory of emotional arousal and have shown the ability to recognize and refute automatic, anger-arousing thoughts. The use of these techniques can be demonstrated by applying them to situations raised by clients.

ASSSERTION TRAINING

As noted earlier, people who have difficulty in containing their anger often alternate in their behavior from passive, sullen withdrawal to outbursts of poorly controlled rage. The intent of assertion training is to provide instruction in an alternative to these two extreme responses to conflict and frustration. Clients are encouraged to have an active rather than a passive response to conflict. They are encouraged to express themselves outwardly rather than to hold things inside until they reach a boiling point.

Assertion training, which consists primarily of behavioral rehearsal, modeling, and role playing a variety of situations in order to enable people to overcome social inhibitions, has been applied to the areas of domestic conflict and anger control by several investigators. Lenore Walker (1979) recommends the use of assertion training with battered women to help overcome learned helplessness. Clarifying personal rights and developing assertive verbal skills enables wives to communicate that they will no longer tolerate abuse. Saunders (1982) suggests the use of assertion training in men's groups to teach skills that are incompatible with aggression, and Rimm, Hill, Brown, and

Stuart (1974) found that group assertion training resulted in a reduction of felt anger for subjects with a history of inappropriate anger and abusive language. Rosenbaum and O'Leary (1981), in comparing groups of husbands from troubled marriages, found that one of the few characteristics that distinguishes abusive husbands from nonabusive husbands is that abusive husbands are significantly less assertive.

Albert Ellis has suggested that hostility and violence often result from a lack of courage. Individuals who fail to confront others may hate themselves for their lack of assertiveness and then become angry and aggressive toward those with whom they acted weakly. He quoted Sherwyn Woods's statement that especially in males, "violence is a restorative act, attempting to restore masculine self-esteem via aggressive demonstrations of power and strength" (Ellis, 1977, p. 110) as compensation for unacceptable feelings of passivity and dependency.

These findings suggest the relevance of assertion training to the treatment of spouse abuse. Although there is considerable overlap between the content, philosophy, and methodology of this program and assertion training, the label "assertion training" should be avoided, as it seems to have potentially frightening connotations for those with a history of poorly controlled anger. Couples have, however, found the distinction between passive, assertive, and aggressive behavior useful in understanding and modifying their interactions. The definitions and consequences of each behavior that follow can be reviewed and referred to when role playing and discussing various problem situations.

Nonassertive Behavior

Nonassertive behavior is an indirect way of getting what we want by manipulating others. Passive behavior allows for the infringement of our rights because of the fear of standing up for them. Passive people may attempt to get their needs met through manipulation, as in the case of the person who claims that nobody cares for him, hoping someone will tell him she does care. A clearer expression of that need might be "Do you care for me?" or "I would like someone to care for me now."

Passive behavior is characterized by nervous, self-effacing gestures and posture, and aims to avoid risky situations by using apologetic words, hedging, and indecisiveness. Passive behavior allows others to make choices for us. The result is that passive people do not get their needs met, or if their needs do get met, it is as a result of other's actions rather than their own. This can lead to anxiety, frustration, and eventually the possibility of an aggressive outburst.

Assertive Behavior

When we act assertively, we take care of our own needs as well as taking into consideration others' needs. Assertive behavior includes being open and direct, expressing feelings as well as thoughts, and may involve persistence on the assertive person's part in cases where others may not be willing to accept the person's choice of behavior.

By being assertive, we also respect others' rights to deny requests. By being able to say no to requests, for example, we can be more understanding when others say no to our requests. Offering and being willing to accept compromises is an important assertive skill and is consistent with attempting to satisfy both individuals' needs.

Assertive behavior is characterized by confident posture and gestures and a strong steady voice. It usually results in feeling good about ourselves. We develop more positive self-concepts because assertive behavior is directed toward meeting our needs, and others respect us for our behavior.

Aggressive Behavior

Aggressive behavior involves attempting to get our needs met without considering the rights of others. It may involve the use of threats or put-downs and usually involves blaming: "*You* didn't do it right" or "*You* made me mad."

This behavior is characterized by rigid posture, pushy gestures, and a raised voice. While aggressive behavior may be effective in getting what we want, in the long run, it may alienate others or make them resentful. Aggressive people may also feel guilty since aggressive behavior is usually emotionally impulsive. In short, friendship and respect may be sacrificed to satisfy immediate needs.

Many people fail to act assertively in their own best interest, not so much because they lack the skill to do so, but because they are not sure they have the *right* to do so. Certain societal values may interfere with people's ability to think clearly about their right to act assertively. The most common messages society gives us that interfere with assertiveness and how they affect our behavior are included in Table 3.

Exercise 7, the Bill of Rights, uses the Bill of Rights Worksheet to help couples discuss the issue of what rights they retain in their relationship and what rights they agree to relinquish as well as pinpoint areas of agreement and disagreement. Exercise 8, Assertiveness Practice, has clients role play situations from their anger logs in order to distinguish between nonassertiveness, assertiveness, and aggressiveness and to practice assertiveness. The Nonassertive, Assertive, and

Table 3

How Socialization Messages May Negatively Affect Assertion

SOCIALIZATION MESSAGE	EFFECT ON RIGHTS	EFFECT ON ASSERTIVE BEHAVIOR	HEALTHY MESSAGE
Think of others first; give to others even if you're hurting. Don't be selfish.	I have no right to place my needs above those of other people.	When I have a conflict with someone else, I will give in and satisfy the other person's needs and forget about my own.	To be selfish means that a person always places her/his needs above other people's. This is undesirable human behavior. All healthy people have needs and strive to fulfill these as much as possible. Your needs are as important as other people's. When there is a conflict over need satisfaction, compromise is a useful way to handle the conflict.
Be modest and humble. Don't act superior to other people.	I have no right to do anything which would imply that I am better than other people.	I will discount my accomplishments and any compliments I receive. When I'm in a meeting, I will encourage other people's contributions and keep silent about my own. When I have an opinion which is different than someone else's, I won't express it; who am I to say that my opinion is better than another's.	It is undesirable to build yourself up at the expense of another person. However, you have as much a right as other people to show your abilities and take pride in yourself. It is healthy to enjoy one's accomplishments.
Be understanding and overlook trivial irritations. Don't be a bitch and complain.	I have no right to express anger or even to feel anger.	When I'm in a line and someone cuts in front of me, I will say nothing. I will not tell my boyfriend that I don't like his constantly interrupting me when I speak.	It is undesirable to deliberately nit pick. However, life is made up of trivial incidents and it is normal to be occasionally irritated by seemingly small events. You have a right to your angry feelings, and if you express them at the time they occur, your feelings won't build up and explode. It is important, however, to express your anger assertively rather than aggressively.

Table 3 (cont.)

SOCIALIZATION MESSAGE	EFFECT ON RIGHTS	EFFECT ON ASSERTIVE BEHAVIOR	HEALTHY MESSAGE
Help other people. Don't be demanding.	I have no right to make requests of other people.	I will not ask my friend to reciprocate babysitting favors.	It is undesirable to incessantly make demands on others. You do have a right to ask someone else to change their behavior if their behavior affects your life in a concrete way.
		I will not ask for a pay increase from my employer.	A request is not the same as a demand. However, if your rights are being violated and your requests for a change are being ignored, you have a right to make demands.
Be sensitive to other people's feelings. Don't hurt other people.	I have no right to do anything which might hurt someone else's feelings or deflate someone else's ego.	I will not say what I really think or feel because that might hurt someone else. I will inhibit my spontaneity so that I don't impulsively say something that would accidentally hurt someone else.	It is undesirable to deliberately try to hurt others. However, it is impossible as well as undesirable to try to govern your life so as to *never* hurt *anyone*. You have a right to express your thoughts and feelings even if someone else's feelings occasionally get hurt. To do otherwise would result in your being phoney and in denying other people an opportunity to learn how to handle their own feelings. Remember that some people get hurt because they're unreasonably sensitive and others use their hurt to manipulate you. If you accidentally hurt someone else, you can generally repair the damage.

Reprinted with permission from P. A. Jakubowski. Assertive behavior and clinical problems of women. In E. I. Rawlings and D. K. Carter (Eds.) *Psychotherapy for Women.* Springfield, Ill.: Charles C. Thomas, 1977, 149–151.

Aggressive Behavior Handout summarizes these behaviors for clients and can be used in Exercise 8.

STRESS-INOCULATION TRAINING

Raymond Novaco (1975) has empirically demonstrated the effectiveness of his stress-inoculation training approach, which combines relaxation, counterconditioning, cognitive restructuring, and self-instruction in developing anger control. Treatment combining all of these elements was found to be superior to either a cognitive only or relaxation only approach.

The term *inoculation* refers to the fact that in this approach the subject is exposed to small, but manageable, levels of stress. This is done by having the client relax and briefly imagine anger-arousing scenes beginning with those involving a low level of annoyance. The Jacobson (1938) relaxation procedures are employed for this purpose.

This treatment model, which consists of cognitive preparation, skill acquisition, and application practice, is clearly detailed in a therapist manual available from Dr. Novaco (1977). Although the approach in its entirety is most appropriate for individual treatment, the cognitive component of self-instruction can be effectively employed with individuals or in a group setting. Here the violence sequence episode is divided into the following stages: preparing for a provocation, impact and confrontation, coping with arousal, and subsequent reflection. Cognitive control is achieved through the use of positive self-statements that are repeated in self-talk at each stage. In addition to the cuing, prompting, and reinforcing values of this procedure, the use of positive self-statements tends to block automatic, irrational self-talk, which might otherwise increase the client's level of arousal.

Clients can formulate their own self-instructions using the examples found in the Anger Management Self-statements Handout, which provide rational self-statements for each of Novaco's stages.

EMPATHY

The ability to empathize has application as an anger-control and conflict-containment technique. Empathy is a complex affective and cognitive process or skill that involves the following components:

1. "Role taking" or the ability to put ourselves mentally in the position of others, portraying their thoughts, feelings, and actions;
2. The ability to distinguish and correctly label or interpret the others' thoughts and feelings; and

3. "Emotional responsiveness" or the ability to be emotionally responsive to others' feelings.

It would seem reasonable to assume that there is a significant negative relationship between empathy and spouse abuse although as yet this has not been empirically investigated. Enhancing the cognitive aspect of empathy (the ability to adopt the perspective of others and recognize their emotional experiences) could result in greater understanding and acceptance of the spouse, thereby reducing the level of conflict and the rate of escalation. In addition, vicariously experiencing the spouse's emotion (expressions of fear and distress) when violence did occur could serve to limit the amount of abuse inflicted on the spouse.

Support for this hypothesis comes from clinical impressions that abusive individuals often display a marked deficit in ability to empathize with their spouses. In cases of severe battering, or when a very high frequency of abuse has been maintained, this deficit in empathy seems to be rather pervasive and enduring. In less serious cases of abuse, the suspension of empathy seems to have been temporarily self-induced in order to permit the violent act to be performed and again later to defend against the experiencing of guilt and remorse.

The cognitive distortions that accompany the experience of anger can be thought of as suspending or rendering ineffective the inhibiting influence of empathy. Labeling, the use of should statements, and mind-reading have the effect of convincing the client that his spouse is a terrible, unjust person (or object) who is deliberately working against him.

It is for these reasons that empathy-related skills training should be considered in the program. Clearly there will be significant individual differences in clients' abilities to profit from this. In those cases where the deficit in empathy is a relatively enduring personality trait, the type and amount of training will be much different from the more benign cases where the suspension of empathy has been temporary and self-induced. Empathy-building techniques include:

1. Role reversal. Role reversal is a role playing technique where couples are asked to switch roles and discuss an issue or respond to a situation in the way they believe their partners would. Its use will enable couples to become aware of each other's perceptions of the conflict situation and permit corrective feedback to occur. Also, by attempting to understand and represent the other's point of view, a spouse is freed from his own perspective and is able to empathetically experience that of his partner.

Role reversal can be employed in an actual role play situation or much more informally during class discussion by simply pausing and asking clients to try to think of how their spouses might have been feeling at the time under discussion. These attempts should always be checked out with the spouse for accuracy and further refinement.

2. Communication skills. The communication skills of *listening*, in which there is a genuine effort to understand and accept the statements and feelings of others, and of *validation*, where point of view and conduct are distinguished from personality and validated or legitimized, both help to develop the ability to empathize. These skills are discussed in Chapter Seven.

3. Accurate empathy. This is the anger-control technique that David Burns (1980) calls the "ultimate anger antidote" (p. 166). Clients can be given instructions on how to catch themselves when they first experience the symptoms of anger. They can learn that this is their discriminative cue signaling that they are beginning to engage in those automatic thoughts, or cognitive distortions, that interfere with the ability to empathize and maintain perspective. If at this point they can learn to focus on the issue rather than the personality, and try to fully understand the spouse's point of view, accurate empathy will be achieved, and the anger will be contained and defused.

Clients may find it difficult to accept the proposition that the moment that they are able to achieve empathy by putting themselves in the other's shoes, their anger will begin to dissipate. This is probably because many people are so used to blaming others and justifying their anger to themselves, which actually fuels additional anger, that they have never experimented with empathy. Although empathy may not lead clients to like or approve of others' behavior, it will make it difficult for them to be intensely angry.

Exercise 9, Empathy, asks clients to role play a conflict situation from their spouses' point of view.

DEALING WITH CRITICISM

When criticized, clients often respond with immediate defensiveness and anger (the counterattack) or by internalizing the other's criticism leading to feelings of hurt, betrayal, and loss of self-esteem. The latter pattern can result in passive/aggressive expressions of anger (retaliation). It is important for clients to keep in mind when dealing with criticism that the critical comments of another, no matter how harsh or unfair, can never directly cause hurt. Only we can put ourselves down by agreeing with and siding with the criticizer.

A more realistic approach for dealing with criticism is to avoid defensiveness and feelings of hurt and see what can be learned from the situation. David Burns (1980) has suggested the following points for dealing with criticism in this way.

1. People's critical comments can be either right or wrong. If the comments are wrong, there is nothing to be particularly upset about— they are simply wrong. It would be unreasonable to expect others' perceptions and opinions to be perfect. If the criticism is right and accurate, there is still no need to be upset as no one is perfect. The error simply should be acknowledged and steps taken to correct it.

2. It is impossible to please all the people all of the time. Self-worth is not dependent on the opinions of others.

3. There is a three-step program for dealing with attacks by others. The first step is to attempt to see the world through the critic's eyes by asking a series of specific questions designed to find out exactly what is meant. This can change an attack into a collaboration of mutual respect. Asking specific questions minimizes the possibility of being rejected totally, creates awareness of specific issues that can be dealt with, and gives the criticizer a day in court. The first step, then, is to respond with empathy by asking specific questions even if you think the criticism is totally unjustified.

The second step is to disarm the critic by finding some way of agreeing whether the critic is right or wrong. The tendency toward self-defense may get in the way of this step. Giving in to this tendency will almost always increase the intensity of the critic's attack. The rules of step two are:

- Find some way to agree with something the critic says.
- Avoid sarcasm or defensiveness.
- Always speak the truth.

Step three involves feedback and negotiation. Once you have listened to the criticism using the empathy method, and disarmed the critic by finding some way of agreeing, explain your position tactfully and assertively, and negotiate any real differences.

Expressing your point of view objectively with the acknowledgment that you might be wrong is a powerful technique for reducing defensiveness. If you complain to yourself, you haven't spoken up enough about your feelings. In those cases where you are wrong, assertively agreeing with criticism, thanking the critic for giving you the feedback, and assertively apologizing for any inconvenience caused can be quite effective. The essential point is to express your position in a nondefensive manner.

Exercise 10 provides a role play for practicing the three-step program for dealing with attacks by others.

AVOIDING ANGER POLLUTION

Exposure to environmental conditions such as watching violent television shows (Surgeon General's Scientific Advisory Committee, 1971; Walters, 1966), witnessing others behave in an aggressive manner (Bandura, 1978), or simply having guns present in the same room (Berkowitz, 1970) can elicit angry thoughts and behavior. It is also possible to relate to certain acquaintances in a consistently negative manner so that their presence prompts critical or unpleasant thoughts. Avoiding these cues or individuals, particularly when clients are susceptible to them, can be an effective means of reducing anger.

HUMOR

Humor reduces aggression-related arousal (Singer, 1968). The arousal of anger almost always involves taking oneself too seriously. Ellis (1977) has suggested that "human disturbance consists largely of overseriousness" (p. 138), and that a good way to combat this tendency is to exaggerate anger-inducing thoughts to the point of absurdity. For example, "Oh, yes, I run the universe and whatever I want has to, in fact immediately has to, come about. Everyone else must live with frustrations and annoyance, but not me" or "I am always perfect. I never treat others unfairly or go back on my promises to them." Humor and exaggeration of automatic anger-producing thoughts can be an effective anger-control technique for clients.

EXPECTING CRAZINESS

Clients can expect people who frequently anger and betray them to continue to act in this unfortunate manner, since they are unlikely to change dramatically in the near future. For example, "What do you expect of someone with a drinking problem—sobriety?" Expecting them to remain pretty much as they are now and not feeling surprised or outraged anew by their conduct can reduce anger.

REWRITING THE RULES

It is easier to change expectations than it is to change the world. People generally act in the way that *they* believe is fair and are unlikely to change simply to suit others. All that clients can probably influence is their own reaction to others' behavior. Thus, rewriting "shoulds" to preferences reduces anger arousal.

FOCUSING ON THE POSITIVE

It is much more effective, as well as more pleasurable, to reward the positive behavior of others rather than punish the negative. Instead of attending in great detail to all the aspects of another's behavior that they don't care for, clients can systematically attend to and reinforce what they do like. Going out of the way to be nice to people they are upset with enables them to practice feeling calm, and may prompt the other people to modify their own behavior.

In a related technique, that of "decentration" (Leyens, Cisneros, & Hossay, 1976), clients are instructed to focus on the positive qualities of an anger-arousing situation that they may have overlooked. Didato (1980) has pointed out that a type of tunnel vision often sets in when we are angry. We focus only on the pain, injustice, or hurt that we are experiencing and disregard all positive thoughts. Decentration involves instructing clients to deliberately broaden their perspective by listing the positive qualities of the target of their anger.

The anger-control techniques that form the basis of this program are not particularly complicated, nor do they require a great deal of sophistication or clinical skill to impart. In fact, the key to the effectiveness of the program has more to do with dogged determination to pursue the clients' automatic, irrational anger-producing thoughts and actively dispute them than it does with subtle clinical skills. In this pursuit, redundancy has its rewards.

Additionally, expressing the key concepts in a form that clients can relate to and adopt as their own without excessive translation can lead to a more rapid assimilation of the program principles. For example, statements like "Anger is a choice," "Expect craziness," and "Think of long-term, not short-term goals" communicate anger-control techniques in a way that clients will understand and remember. Clients will begin to repeat these phrases in subsequent discussions and use them when controlling their anger.

EXERCISE 7

BILL OF RIGHTS

Distribute the Bill of Rights Worksheet and ask that each couple work together to complete it. Couples should not expect to get perfect agreement and the focus should be directed more toward those items where there is agreement than toward those where agreement does not occur. Considerable discussion is generally required as the statements are open to a variety of interpretations. The purpose is to present the idea that there are definite rights that individuals retain and there are certain rights that individuals agree to relinquish within an ongoing relationship.

EXERCISE 8

ASSERTIVENESS PRACTICE

In order to practice distinguishing between nonassertive, assertive, and aggressive response patterns and to practice assertiveness, have clients select incidents from their anger logs and role play examples of the three ways of responding. If done in a group, other clients can evaluate the performance using the Nonassertive, Assertive, and Aggressive Behavior Handout. Situations that were raised during checking in could also be assigned to the group to role play.

Clients can evaluate their own performance in the role play by responding to the following questions:

1. Do you feel satisfied with the level of assertion you demonstrated?
2. What were your rights in the situation?
3. What were the rights of the other party?
4. Did you engage in positive rehearsal and self-talk?
5. Did you respond directly, openly, and without defensiveness or aggression?
6. Did you consider the consequences of your behavior to yourself and to the other person?
7. Is there any additional action you would like to take?

EXERCISE 9

EMPATHY

Have clients role play a conflict situation from the spouse's point of view. This can be done with a conflict situation volunteered during checking in. For example:

> Bob is furious to discover upon returning home that the breakfast dishes still have not been washed. He enrages himself by telling himself that his wife is totally lazy and once again has deliberately chosen to disobey his request in order to prove her independence. He ignores her statements that she had to wait in the doctor's office all afternoon for their son to be seen.
>
> When asked to assume his wife's role in a demonstration of empathy, he realized how frustrating it must have been for her to spend her day at the doctor's office and that, rather than a deliberate gesture of defiance, she chose not to do the dishes because other things were more important to do.

EXERCISE 10

DEALING WITH CRITICISM

Ask clients to follow the three-step program for dealing with attacks by others, using situations that are appropriate for your clients and that will not provoke undue hostility between spouses. For example, have wives respond to a comment such as "Why can't you cook decent food anymore!" Ask husbands to respond to a comment such as "You never help around the house. *I* have to do everything!"

> Remind clients to (1) ask specific questions to clarify exactly what the spouse means, (2) disarm the spouse by finding some way of agreeing whether the spouse is right or wrong, and (3) provide feedback and negotiate any real differences.

BILL OF RIGHTS WORKSHEET

Read through the following list of rights and indicate:

    A = We agree that the husband has this right.
    B = We agree that the wife has this right.
    C = We agree that both have this right.
    D = We agree to disagree.

_____ The right to be treated with respect

_____ The right to constructively express feelings and opinions

_____ The right to be listened to and taken seriously

_____ The right to ask for what is wanted

_____ The right to show feelings and express fears

_____ The right to say no

_____ The right to reject stereotypes and to set own standards

_____ The right to live without fear of abuse

_____ The right to have friends and outside interests

_____ The right to make mistakes and accept responsibilities for errors and shortcomings

_____ The right not to be perfect

_____ The right to privacy and time alone

_____ The right to be treated like an adult

_____ The right to say "I don't know"

_____ The right to say "I disagree"

_____ The right to not make excuses

_____ The right to change decisions

NONASSERTIVE, ASSERTIVE, AND AGGRESSIVE BEHAVIOR HANDOUT

	NONASSERTIVE BEHAVIOR	ASSERTIVE BEHAVIOR	AGGRESSIVE BEHAVIOR
CHARACTERISTICS OF THE BEHAVIOR	Ignores, does not express own rights, needs, desires. Permits others to infringe on rights. Emotionally dishonest, indirect, inhibited, manipulative. Self-denying. Allows others to choose.	Expresses and asserts own rights, needs. Stands up for legitimate rights in a way that does not violate rights of others. Emotionally honest, direct, expressive. Self-enhancing. Persistent. Chooses for self.	Expresses own rights at expense of others. Inappropriate outburst or hostile overreaction. Intent to humiliate, to get even, to put the other down. Self-enhancing. Chooses for others.
YOUR FEELINGS WHEN YOU ENGAGE IN THIS BEHAVIOR	Internalized, weak, hurt, anxious. Disappointed in self at the time and possibly angry later.	Stated, confident, self-respecting. Feels good about self at the time and later.	Externalized, angry, righteous, indignant. Feels superior, possibly guilty later.
NONVERBAL BEHAVIOR	Downcast, averted, darting or teary eyes. Shifting of weight, slumped body, round shoulders, head down, shuffling. Wringing of hands, biting lips, adjusting clothing, nervous gestures. Pleading, monotone, apologetic, mumbling, whining, hesitant, giggly voice.	Open, direct, not staring eye contact. Standing comfortably but firmly on two feet, steady, straight. Hands loosely at sides, relaxed. Strong, steady, firm, clear tone of voice.	Glaring, narrowed, expressionless eyes. Leaning forward, stiff, rigid posture. Clenched fists, jerky movements, finger pointing, hands on hips. Raised, snickering, haughty tone of voice.

NONASSERTIVE, ASSERTIVE, AND AGGRESSIVE BEHAVIOR HANDOUT (cont.)

	NONASSERTIVE BEHAVIOR	ASSERTIVE BEHAVIOR	AGGRESSIVE BEHAVIOR
GENERAL POSTURE	Moving away, self-effacing, dependent.	Moving toward, facing up to situations, standing up for self, independent or interdependent.	Moving against, other-effacing, counter-dependent.
VERBAL BEHAVIOR	Rambling statements. Qualifiers (maybe/I wonder if you could/only just). Fillers (uh/well/you know). Negatives (Don't bother/It's not important).	Concise statements. "I" statements (I think/I feel/I want). Cooperative words (Let's/How can we resolve this?). Empathic statements of interest (What do you think?/What do you see?).	Clipped, interrupting statements. Threats (you'd better/if you don't/watch out). Calling names, demanding, accusing. Put-downs (Come on/You must be kidding). Judgmental, sarcastic, evaluative.
OUTCOME	Does not achieve desired goals.	May achieve desired goals.	Achieves desired goals by hurting others.
PAYOFF	Avoids unpleasant and risky situations, avoids conflict. Doesn't get needs met. Accumulates anger. Feels nonvalued.	Feels good, valued by self and others. Feels better about self, improves self-confidence. Needs are met, relationships are freer.	Saves up anger, resentment justifies a blow-up, an emotional outburst, "to get even, get back at."

Adapted from: J. William Pfeiffer and John E. Jones, Eds., *The 1976 Annual Handbook for Group Facilitators*, San Diego, CA: University Associates, Inc., 1976. Used with permission.

ANGER MANAGEMENT SELF-STATEMENTS HANDOUT

PREPARING FOR A PROVOCATION

This may be upsetting, but I know how to cope.
Remember, lose your cool and you lose control.
Stick to the issue; don't take it personally.
Nobody can *make* me mad; it's up to me.
Take that deep breath, hold it, exhale, and relax.

IMPACT AND CONFRONTATION

I'm cool and in control.
Stay calm. Continue to relax.
Control my thinking and control my anger.
It would be nice if she didn't act like that.
There's no reason to get angry.

COPING WITH AROUSAL

Tight muscles? Stay loose and relax.
Time to take a deep breath.
There is no payoff in getting angry.
Stick to the issue and ride it through.
Anger is a signal that I need to take control of myself.
She might like me to lose it, but I'm in control.
It would be nice if people were the way I want them to be.
Let me see it through her eyes and empathize.
Cool thoughts for hot.

SUBSEQUENT REFLECTION

I kept my cool and I kept control.
I made it. Now stick with the cool.
I'm getting better and better.
Write it down. Another success.
It could have been a lot worse.

Chapter Six

Stress and Violence

Violence tends to be precipitated by stress and conflict. Straus (1980) has reported a significant relationship between a number of stressful conditions and violence between spouses. In our own studies, the Life Events Scale, a modification of the Holmes and Rahe Social Readjustment Rating Scale (Holmes & Rahe, 1967), was used as a measure of the amount of stressful experiences dealt with by clients. Those subjects involved in domestic violence received an average score of 416 as compared to 260 for the nonviolent subjects (Friedman, Note 4). Spouse abuse generally occurs during periods of high stress for the couple. Various measures of stress are predictive of the frequency, but not necessarily the severity, of violent episodes. This chapter considers the measurement of stress and the factors that contribute to the likelihood that people under stress will engage in violent behavior. The stressors specific to the military environment are also discussed. Stress-management strategies are presented to help clients recognize and deal with stress.

It is helpful for clients to be introduced to stress management with a detailed presentation of the relationship between the amount of stress they experience, predisposing variables, and violence for the following reasons:

1. It provides them with a theoretical model for understanding their own violent behavior.
2. The model is well supported empirically, that is, it is *believable*, and it is one that engenders motivation and hope because it is acceptable. Clients are readily able to acknowledge that they are under a high level of pressure and are relieved that violence is not considered to be either innate or a sign of severe pathology.
3. The model suggests intervention or positive change strategies, and the relevance of stress-management training for controlling violence becomes apparent.

THE MEASUREMENT OF STRESS

Obviously there is an infinite variety of stressful events or stressors that individuals may experience. It is also obvious that what is stressful for one person will not necessarily be stressful for other people. As Hans Selye has noted (1974), it can be just as stressful for a racehorse to have to act as a turtle as it is for a turtle to have to perform like a racehorse. In spite of these individual differences, Table 4, Scores for the Life Events Scale, makes several important points about stress.

Table 4

Scores for the Life Events Scale

86	1.	Death of spouse
30	2.	Trouble with superiors at work
26	3.	Trouble with other people at work
70	4.	Divorce or marital separation
60	5.	Death of close friend or family member
50	6.	Marriage or marital reconciliation
31	7.	Changes in hours or working conditions
34	8.	Minor law violation (traffic tickets, disturbing the peace, etc.)
49	9.	Pregnancy (or wife's pregnancy)
26	10.	Quarrel with neighbors
38	11.	Involvement in a fight outside the home
43	12.	Increase in number of arguments with spouse
40	13.	Increase in arguments or problems with other family members (in-laws or children)
59	14.	Problems with alcohol or drugs
75	15.	Arrest or charge for something serious
34	16.	Disciplinary action at work
40	17.	Financial problems or debts
59	18.	Serious sickness or injury
40	19.	Serious health problem of close family member
57	20.	Sexual difficulties
40	21.	Move to different neighborhood or town
49	22.	Child in trouble at school or with the law
20	23.	Change in number of family get-togethers
25	24.	Change in sleeping habits
27	25.	Major change in type or amount of recreation
41	26.	Separation from spouse due to work or travel
34	27.	Wife beginning or ending work
31	28.	Poor fitness report or evaluation
43	29.	New baby
30	30.	Children in home under age 3

Adapted with permission from the *Journal of Psychosomatic Research,* 11, T. H. Holmes & R. H. Rahe, The social readjustment rating scale, Copyright 1967, Pergamon Press, Ltd.

The original scale was developed by Holmes and Rahe (1967) by compiling a list of common life-change events that people are likely to experience that require adaptation. Some of the events are generally considered to be positive and some negative, but they all involve a drain of energy and resources. Each event was then assigned a weighting that represented the amount of change required to cope with it as estimated through interviews with a large sample of people. Marriage was arbitrarily assigned a weighting of 50 points, and subjects rated the other events in terms of how much adjustment each required in comparison to marriage. The Life Events Scale kept the original weightings as much as possible, but substituted events that are more likely to be experienced by abusive couples.

Holmes and Rahe developed their table in order to predict health changes on the basis of life events. They considered scores of approximately 150 points or less to be normal. They found that about 10 percent of people scoring in this range will have a health change (illness, accident, or psychiatric condition) serious enough to require hospitalization at some time during the following 2 years. For those scoring 150–199, they found that about 37 percent will have a serious health change. For those scoring 200–299, there is a 50 percent chance; between 300–399, an 80 percent chance; and for those scoring above 350, a 90 percent chance of a serious health change was found.

The point of discussing measurements of stress is not so much to enable clients to predict their likelihood of experiencing health problems but to help them recognize that stressful events affect everybody, that some events are more stressful than others, and that we all have a limited capacity for dealing with stressful events. It can also be pointed out that even those events that are generally considered to be desirable (e.g., having a baby, getting married) are stressful in that they require effort and energy, and that the effects of stress are cumulative. Thus, it is best not to make a number of moves or decisions requiring major change in a short period of time. High levels of stress increase the potential for violent conflict. When facing stress, people whose background predisposes them to violence are much more likely to act out their stress, while other people are likely to internalize their stress and are therefore susceptible to physical illness.

INTERVENING VARIABLES IN STRESS AND VIOLENCE

In his investigation of the relationship between stress and violence Straus (1980a) concluded that stress does not directly cause violence. In his study, most people who experienced a high level of stress were not violent. Violence is just one of a number of possible responses to stress. Other possible responses include physical illness, alcoholism, depression, mental illness, and flight. Relationships between these response patterns and levels of stress have also been demonstrated. It is only when stress occurs in the presence of certain intervening or predisposing factors that violence is likely to occur.

Straus (1980a) has conceptualized stress as a mediating variable that must occur in combination with one or more other factors in order for violence to be initiated. Once violence occurs, a feedback loop is established that increases the potential for further violence. For example, a high level of conflict and stress in the family combined with the husband's belief that it is legitimate to use violence on family members who "do wrong" and "won't listen to reason" can lead to a high rate of violence and spouse abuse. This high rate of violence reinforces the husband's belief that the use of violence is legitimate and, in turn, leads to more violence.

Among men reporting the same high level of stress, Straus found several variables that predisposed some of the men to violence. For example, those men whose fathers had never hit their mothers had an assault rate on their own wives of 5.4 incidents a year per 100 husbands, while among those men whose fathers had hit their mothers, the assault rate rose to 17.1 incidents per 100 men. Similarly, the assault rate for men who participated in organizational activities frequently (11 or more times per year) had an assault rate of 1.7 per 100 men, while those who never participated had a rate of 10.5 assaults. The predisposing factors are not sufficient in themselves to cause violence to occur but seem to act to determine the individual's ability to deal constructively with provocation. Table 5 lists some of the intervening variables identified by Straus.

Although comparable data were not presented for women, Straus did state that "in the absence of stress, women are less violent to their spouse than are men, but under stressful conditions, women are more violent" (Straus, 1980a, p. 240).

The amount of stress that clients are experiencing and the factors that might predispose them to violence should be discussed including these points:

1. Recognizing the influence of early experiences on current behavior;
2. Recognizing the stress levels and predisposing factors that may put them at risk for violence;

Table 5

Effect of Intervening Variables on the
Incidence of Assault by Husbands Experiencing High Stress

INTERVENING VARIABLE	Assault Rate per 100 Husbands when Intervening Variable Was:	
	LOW	HIGH
Husband's father hit his mother (0 vs. 1+ per yr.)	5.4	17.1
Husband's mother hit his father (0 vs. 1+ per yr.)	4.6	23.5
Approval of slapping a spouse (0 vs. any approval)	2.7	15.0
Marital satisfaction index (low vs. high quartile)	12.3	4.9
Power norm index (high = husband should have final say)	4.2	16.3
Decision power index (high = husband has final say)	5.2	16.1
Organizational participation index (0 vs. 11+)	10.5	1.7

Adapted with permission from M. A. Straus. Social stress and marital violence in a national sample of American families. *Annals of the New York Academy of Science,* 1980, *347,* 243.

3. Understanding that simply because they are at risk, violence is not inevitable;
4. Recognizing how predisposing factors and high stress can be managed.

MILITARY STRESSORS

Certain types of stressors particularly affect clients in the military. Many military men are so immersed in the military environment that they are unable to detect the influence of this environment on their lives. In discussing the specific stressors inherent in the military community, a problem-solving focus should be maintained. This will avoid potentially divisive situations such as being placed in a position of defending the establishment, having wives start complaining about and husbands defending the military, and losing the problem-solving or lump-it-gracefully intent through extended griping.

Zais and Taylor (1982), in an article on stress and the military, have pointed out that the military ethic has consistently valued mission accomplishment over individual welfare. The military emphasizes physical and mental rigor, a Spartan orientation, and the unlimited ability and dedication of the soldier. Implications of this ethic for the family are very important.

There is a pervasive emphasis in the military community on team work and on the importance of the primary group working together. Under controlled conditions, this cohesiveness and group identity would provide the support and strength to survive conditions that might defeat the individual. A deliberate effort on the part of the military is made to foster this group identity through drills, athletic events, living and eating together, and socializing as a group. This group emphasis, which is adaptive for combat conditions, may contribute to wives' feeling excluded and unimportant. The fact that this membership is male dominated with its own language, uniform, and set of priorities may heighten this sense of alienation for the wives. The often heard quip "If the Marine Corps (or any other service branch) had wanted you to have a wife, they would have issued you one" is felt by many wives to reflect the military's feelings toward them. The term *dependent,* which has been used to refer to wives and children, further reinforces this perception.

The military emphasis on "mission accomplishment" frequently leads to long work hours with no additional compensation that intrude into family time. There may be periods of relative idleness interrupted by times of urgency ("hurry up and wait"). Task overload, competition, and role ambiguity are not unique to the military, but often exert considerable pressure.

The regimentation and lack of privacy found in the military community, and particularly in military housing, often result in intrusions by authorities into areas of family life far beyond what is found in the civilian community. Men may be called on to control their wives and children or be held directly responsible for their families' conduct. This dictate strongly suggests that the authoritarian model of the workplace should also be applied in the home.

The hierarchical and authoritarian model, with its clearly established chain of command, rank structure, and communication in the form of decisive commands, works quite well in the military setting. However, this same model creates considerable conflict when it is attempted within the family. Wives and children are not subordinates, and unquestioning obedience should not be the standard in a family.

The frequent relocation required by the service disrupts support networks and contributes to isolation, especially for wives. Low pay may also lead to isolation, particularly in the lower ranks.

Finally, the prevailing ethic in military communities of self-sufficiency and machismo reinforces the belief that anyone who experiences problems is not manly and should be weeded out. This belief tends to isolate those who are experiencing problems and makes it difficult for them to admit, even to their family or friends, that they are in trouble.

There seems to be a link between stress and domestic violence in the military. This is suggested in a study by Shwed and Straus (Note 10) in which they analyzed confirmed cases of child abuse within the Air Force. They found that child abuse was somewhat more frequent in the military than in the civilian community and that, contrary to the pattern in civilian populations, fathers tended to be more abusive than mothers. The stress-related factors found to be linked to higher incidence of child abuse were geographical isolation, low rank, and military duty or job description associated with violence.

Those males who have engaged in violence directed against their spouses report significantly higher levels of stress than nonabusive service personnel (Friedman, Note 8). The report *Wife Abuse in the Armed Forces* (West, Turner, & Dunwoody, 1981) calls for additional supporting research on the conceptualization of domestic violence as a learned behavior.

Stress reduction for clients in the military involves recognizing the conflict between their military and family roles and building barriers between these roles. The type of authoritarian, critical, impersonal behavior that may be encountered in the military work setting conflicts with the more democratic, warm, and intimate behavior important in the family. Barriers between these roles can include establishing a good range of nonmilitary interests and friends, confining any work that needs to be done at home to one room of the house, or unwinding after work before joining the family by stopping for a cup of coffee or engaging in a solitary activity like jogging or reading.

Exercise 11, The Good Soldier Versus the Good Husband/Parent, asks clients to describe the difference between the two roles in part A, and discusses how they can create some barriers between their work and home lives in part B.

STRESS-MANAGEMENT TRAINING

Stress can be thought of as an imbalance between the client's coping ability and the demands placed on him by his environment. "Stressors" are the events that require adaptive efforts, and "stress symptoms" or "stress reactions" are the adverse effects of exposure to high levels of environmental pressure. In the stress-management training model that follows (Neidig, Note 11), clients learn to identify their stress symptoms, identify stressors contributing to their symptoms, acquire coping skills and develop a plan for dealing with stress, and, finally, implement their stress management plan. This is shown in Figure 1.

Figure 1. Stress-management model

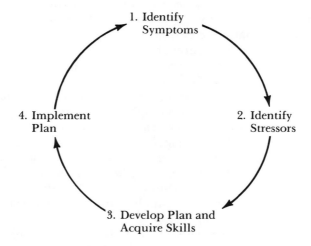

From P. H. Neidig. *Stress management manual.* Unpublished manuscript, 1982.

Identify Symptoms

Response to stress is nonspecific; that is, our bodies generally respond to all types of stress in the same way. The symptoms of stress, however, may be different for each of us. Stress symptoms can be physical (headache, tightness of the chest, rapid breathing); psychological (depression, irritability, apathy); or behavioral (sleep disturbance, excessive use of alcohol, restlessness).

How we interpret these symptoms or the label we apply to our reactions will in large part determine our emotional response. For example, if I label my state of arousal (rapid breathing, tense muscles, etc.) as anger, I will feel angry, but if I label it as fear, I will feel fearful. The implications of this attribution, or labeling process, are detailed in Chapter Four, Anger Control.

The tendency we all inherited to respond to stress is healthy or adaptive in the sense that it enables us to run faster or fight harder than we would normally be able to (the fight or flight syndrome). Of course, most contemporary stressors cannot be taken care of by running or fighting as may have been the case previously in our history.

It is only when stress is excessive that these fight/flight stress responses begin to create difficulties. For example, tense muscles, which enable us to react quickly, cause cramps, headaches, backache, and fatigue when prolonged. An increased heart rate, which sends more blood and oxygen to our tissues, can, over time, cause high blood pressure, stroke, or heart attack. Further examples of the negative effects of stress can be found in Table 6.

Discussion of stress symptoms can do much to dispel the fallacy of uniqueness—the tendency to view others as doing just fine and only ourselves as weak or suffering. This perception of stress symptoms as a sign of weakness that must be concealed and denied is quite common among abusive males and contributes significantly to the tension-building phase of the cycle of violence. Self-disclosure in this area seems to be facilitated by the understanding that everyone can tolerate just so much pressure and that symptomatic behavior, at least when linked to an identifiable external stressor, is acceptable. There is a tendency, however, to lose sight of this knowledge during periods of high stress and to withdraw and negatively evaluate ourselves when we most need the support of others.

Stress symptoms serve the function of an early warning system, signaling that some sort of adjustment is required. If we experience chronic, high levels of stress, we may adapt to some of these signals and fail to take action on them. Or, we may mask symptoms through the use of alcohol or medications. Having to drink three alcoholic drinks before being able to relax after work or falling asleep in front of the TV each evening before dinner is not considered normal and should not be ignored. A drop in the level of symptoms will signal when efforts at stress management are paying off.

The harmful effects of prolonged stress can be discussed using Table 6. Exercise 12, Stress Symptom Generation, uses the Stress Symptoms Handout to help clients identify their own stress symptoms. This exercise can be especially powerful in a group setting. Listening to others express their stress symptoms helps clients realize that it is normal to be affected by stress. This makes it easier for clients to recognize and articulate their feelings, and it also builds a sense of sharing in the group.

Identify Stressors

Once clients have identified their own unique stress symptoms and understand the importance of symptoms as signals to take action, they can go on to identify stressors, or factors contributing to stress levels.

Table 6

Short-term and Long-term Effects of Stress on the Body

BODY CHANGE	ACTION OR SHORT-TERM EFFECT	POTENTIAL LONG-TERM EFFECT
Tense muscles	Quick reaction	Headache; back, neck, shoulder, and jaw pain; fatigue
Restricted flow of blood to skin	Blood diverted to other areas to minimize blood loss in injury	Pallor; skin rashes; itching, dryness
Increased perspiration	Cools body	Loss of fluids; body odor
Blood clotting mechanism activated	Minimizes blood loss in injury	Blood clots; stroke; heart attack
Increased production of white blood cells	Fights infection	Immune system becomes unbalanced
Increased heart rate	Increased flow of blood carrying oxygen and nutrients	High blood pressure; irregular heart sounds; rapid heart rate; damage to heart muscle
Increased respiratory rate	Provides more oxygen; eliminates carbon dioxide	Impaired breathing; hyperventilation
Digestion depressed	Blood diverted to other areas where needed	Nausea; indigestion; colitis; diarrhea
Increase of acid in stomach	Irritates stomach lining	Ulcers
Decrease in saliva	Not needed for digestion	Dry mouth; indigestion; loss of voice
Liver releases extra sugar	More energy available	Diabetes
Increase of fatty acids and cholesterol	More energy available	Cholesterol buildup in arteries; stroke; heart attack
Pupils dilate	Increased visual perception	Impaired vision

Adapted from Figure 3.18 from *Stress for success* by D. Morse. Copyright © 1979 by Van Nostrand Reinhold Co. Inc.
Reprinted by permission of the publisher.

It is very important to introduce the idea that particular stressors do not have an identical effect on all people. Interaction between the events in our environment and our perception or definition of those events creates the stress response. Anger is just one of a number of possible responses to stress, depending on a person's labeling and stress-management skills.

It is also important when identifying stressors to be as precise as possible, defining events in specific, operational terms rather than using global labels. It may require considerable practice for clients to develop this skill. For example, rather than thinking, "That jerk, my boss, is my stressor," they should specify, "I experience stress when my boss blames me for something that was not my responsibility in the first place." Or, rather than "My wife is lazy," specify, "I experience stress when I come home after working all day and my wife is still wearing her robe."

Stressors can be defined as "possible stressors" (those that can be influenced or changed by the individual) or "impossible stressors" (those that are beyond control or influence). Possible, changeable stressors can be further categorized as:

1. Internal. Internal stressors are mostly self-inflicted due to the individual's values or standards, or to the way in which the stressor has been perceived by the individual. For example: "I must be perfect." "Everyone must like me." "All my subordinates must respect me." "My house must be spotless." "The children have to do well in school."

2. External-interpersonal. These have to do with relating to others. For example: making the children obey, getting along with spouse, asking boss for time off, dealing with bothersome neighbors, getting spouse to do chores.

3. External-impersonal. These stressors have very little to do with people but are more a result of environmental conditions or equipment. For example: extended hours, excessive noise, or fast pace at work; problems with the car; crowded living conditions.

The skills of identifying, defining, and categorizing stressors will not be of any benefit to clients unless they are systematically practiced. Exercise 13, Stressor Identification, helps clients to do this. The Irrational Beliefs Handout can be distributed to aid in identifying common beliefs that contribute to internally generated stress and to provide rational thoughts to counter them.

Plan and Acquire Skills

Once a stressor has been identified and defined in specific operational terms, it is usually not very difficult to develop a plan for dealing with it. Frequently the process of putting the stressor into clear, relatively unemotional terms will help achieve a more reasonable perspective and result in some reduction of stress. Stressors and conflicts do not have to be thoroughly resolved before the clients can experience some relief.

For those stressors that are defined as "impossible," just the process of recognizing that they are beyond the clients' limits of responsibility may reduce the sense of urgency and pressure. This is the important skill of distinguishing what is impossible to change from what is merely very difficult and then learning to "lump it gracefully."

It should be emphasized that simply identifying, labeling, and expressing stress symptoms and being able to put stressors into operational terms constitutes a significant accomplishment. People involved in spouse abuse often have considerable difficulty in admitting their shortcomings, in correctly articulating their feelings, and in being self-disclosing.

Much of this book is devoted to skill acquisition activities intended to increase ability to cope with stress (relaxation training, communication skills, conflict containment, anger control). Table 7 indicates which intervention approaches are most appropriate for each type of stressor. Going through this table with clients serves to emphasize the relevance of the program content to their particular concerns. In a group setting, it is valuable to know what types of stressors are common to group members so that the content of treatment can be adapted to meet the group's needs.

Implement Plan

If clients experience difficulties at the implementation stage it is usually because:

1. They have failed to define the problem in specific operational terms so that it still looks impossible.
2. They have not broken the problem down into small enough steps.
3. They have attempted to change too many things at one time.
4. They have not stuck with the change process long enough for positive effects to occur.
5. They have not paid enough attention to the gradual but steady improvement they have made to experience sufficient reward for their efforts.

Table 7
Intervention Strategies for Different Types of Stressors

TYPE OF STRESSOR	TECHNIQUE OR STRATEGY
Internal	Relaxation Training A-B-C Anger Control Recognizing Irrational Beliefs
External-interpersonal	Assertion Training Dealing with Criticism Communication Skills Conflict Containment
External-impersonal	Stress-Inoculation Training Relaxation Training
Impossible (Unchangeable)	Relaxation Training Social Support Network

Offer assurances that assistance will be available and that none of these potential difficulties is insurmountable.

RELAXATION TRAINING

The skills that can be acquired through relaxation training have two primary applications. First, as a technique of stress management, relaxation training is a thoroughly researched, effective means of lowering the general tension level. Borkovec, Grayson, and Cooper (1978) reported that a progressive muscle relaxation training program resulted in a significant decline in self-report measures of tension for a group of highly tense subjects and that these gains were maintained over a 5-month follow-up. The second application of relaxation skills is in the area of anger control. Novaco (1978) found that subjects in a laboratory provocation situation who learned relaxation, particularly when coupled with cognitive coping instructions, were able to demonstrate increased self-control over anger as measured by self-report and physiological indices.

Progressive relaxation training consists of learning to tense and relax muscle groups throughout the body and learning to recognize the feelings associated with both tension and relaxation (Jacobson, 1938). The goal of relaxation training in this program is to teach clients to consciously reduce tension during times of stress.

In learning the relaxation procedures, clients will be able to:

1. Lower their baseline level of tension;
2. Detect changes in bodily tension promptly to permit the use

of coping strategies before the tension level becomes problematic;

3. Use relaxation to cope with specific provocations and stressors.

It is important when introducing relaxation training that the rationale be thoroughly explained. The Relaxation Instructions in Exercise 13 can be used for this purpose with supplemental information available in *Progressive Relaxation Training* by Bernstein and Borkovec (1973). Clients need to be receptive, motivated, and have enough trust in the therapist and group members (if any) to participate in the initial demonstration. Russell and Gribble (1982) have pointed out that a good deal of flexibility is required when working with overcontrolled clients who have a high level of mistrust and concern about maintaining control over themselves. Some of the procedural modifications required for this population could include not dimming the lights; being careful to maintain a conversational tone when delivering instructions; having subjects sit upright; and permitting subjects to practice in the security of their own homes.

In the interest of time, the demonstration and entire progressive relaxation procedure is usually not repeated more than once or twice in the treatment sessions. However, clients are encouraged to practice at home and, particularly, to apply relaxation to anger-arousing situations. Once the relaxation training approach has been introduced, it is helpful to begin each subsequent session with a couple of minutes of deep breathing exercises (found in Chapter Four, Exercise 5). These serve to enable participants to shift from their workday orientations and also reinforce the value of relaxation in coping with stress.

Exercise 14, Relaxation, uses the Relaxation Instructions to explain the rationale of relaxation training to clients and takes them through a relaxation session with the Relaxation Script.

EXERCISE 11

**THE GOOD SOLDIER VERSUS
THE GOOD HUSBAND/PARENT**

A. Ask clients to generate a list of words that describe the attitudes, values, and behavior of a good soldier and of a good husband and father and list these on the board. Examples:

GOOD SOLDIER	GOOD HUSBAND/FATHER
Authoritarian	Democratic
Automatic obedience	Eventual independence
Punishes	Rewards
Strong and decisive	Human and responsive
Criticizes	Compliments
Issues orders	Requests
Dictates	Encourages
Impersonal	Intimate
Closed	Sharing

B. Ask couples to discuss how they can create barriers between work and home to help minimize the stressful effects of role incompatibility. What kinds of transition rituals can be used to help in unwinding and shifting roles? Examples:

1. Don't wear the uniform or other military gear at home.
2. Establish a good range of nonmilitary interests and friends.
3. Confine discussions about work to the first 30 minutes after getting home from work.
4. If work needs to be done at home, confine it to one room of the house.
5. Take 30 minutes to read the paper, jog, work in the yard, or do some other solitary activity before entering into the activities of the family.
6. Stop on the way home for a cup of coffee.

EXERCISE 12

STRESS SYMPTOM GENERATION

Ask clients to think of four or five ways in which they usually respond to stress—the symptoms they generally experience. The symptoms clients name should include physical symptoms, psychological symptoms, and behavioral symptoms. The Stress Symptoms Handout will prompt clients. In a group setting, these symptoms should be listed on the board and common stress reactions should be emphasized to reduce any sense of weakness and uniqueness.

EXERCISE 13

STRESSOR IDENTIFICATION

Ask clients to think of three or four stressors (events that create the most stress and difficulty for them) and to try to translate them into specific, operational terms. Once a list has been made, have them identify those stressors that are considered most stressful. Attempt to divide the list into possible stressors and impossible stressors. Further categorize the list of possible, changeable stressors into internal, external-interpersonal, and external-impersonal. Distribute the Irrational Beliefs Handout to help clients identify common beliefs that contribute to internally generated stress.

EXERCISE 14

RELAXATION

Explain the rationale of relaxation training using the Relaxation Instructions. Demonstrate the tense-relax approach by having clients get comfortable in their chairs with both feet resting on the floor and arms supported either on their laps or on the chair arms. Ask them to close their eyes, breathe deeply once or twice, then tighten the muscles of one hand, wrist, and forearm by clenching the fist and holding it for 5 seconds, finally relaxing or letting go of the tension all at once. Then ask them to clench and relax the muscles of the other hand and arm. Direct attention to the sensations that accompany relaxation.

Following this demonstration, go through the entire progressive relaxation procedure using the Relaxation Script. Taped relaxation instructions can be used and provided to participants for practice at home. Research has generally supported the effectiveness of relaxation training through the use of audio tapes even though live administration is typically found to be superior (Borkovec & Sides, 1979).

Relaxation Instructions

The technique we have been discussing to reduce your tension is called progressive relaxation. It was first developed in the 1930s by a physiologist named Jacobson, and in recent years it has been modified to be simpler and more effective. Basically, progressive relaxation training consists of learning to sequentially tense and then relax various groups of muscles all through the body, while at the same time paying very close and careful attention to the feelings associated with both tension and relaxation. Then, in addition to learning to relax, you will also be taught to recognize and pinpoint tension and relaxation as they appear in everyday situations as well as in our sessions here.

Learning relaxation skills is very much like learning any other kind of skill such as swimming, golfing, or riding a bicycle; in order for you to get better at relaxing, you need to practice doing it just as you would practice other skills. It is very important that you realize that relaxation training involves learning on your part; there is nothing magical about the procedures. Thus, without your *active cooperation* and *regular practice* of the things you will learn, the procedures are of little use.

You will be asked to tense and then relax various groups of muscles in your body. You may be wondering why, if we want to produce relaxation, we start off by producing tension. The reason is that, first of all, we are always at some level of tension during our waking hours; if we were not tense to some extent, we would simply fall down. The amount of tension actually present in everyday life differs, of course, from individual to individual, and we say that each person has reached some adaptation level—the amount of tension under which that person operates day to day.

The goal of relaxation training is to help you learn to reduce muscle tension in your body far below your adaptation level at any time you wish to do so. In order to accomplish this, you could focus your attention, for example, on the muscles in your right hand and lower arm and then just let them relax. Now you might think that

EXERCISE 14 (cont.)

you can let these muscles drop down below their adaptation level just by letting them go, and to a certain extent, you probably can. However, in relaxation, we want you to learn to produce larger and very much more noticeable reductions in tension and the best way to do this is first to produce a good deal of tension in the muscle group (raise the tension well above adaptation level) and then, all at once, release that tension. The release creates a "momentum" that allows the muscles to drop well below adaptation level. The effect is like that which we could produce with a pendulum. If it were hanging motionless in a vertical position and we wanted it to swing far to the right, we could push it quite hard in that direction. It would be much easier, however, to start by pulling the pendulum in the opposite direction and then letting it go. It would swing well past the vertical point and continue in the direction we wanted it to go.

Thus, tensing muscle groups prior to letting them relax is like giving ourselves a "running start" toward deep relaxation through the momentum created by the tension release. Another important advantage of creating and releasing tension is that it will give you a good chance to *focus your attention upon and become clearly aware of what tension really feels like in each of the various groups of muscles we will be dealing with today.* In addition, the tensing procedure will make a vivid contrast between tension and relaxation and will give you an excellent opportunity to directly compare the two and appreciate the difference in feeling associated with each of these states.

The importance of practicing at home cannot be overemphasized. Relaxation is a skill that needs to be practiced if it is to improve. We encourage you to practice *every day,* twice a day, for periods of about 20 minutes each time.

There are several conditions necessary for successful home practice:

1. A comfortable chair that supports your head and arms, or a bed;
2. A place where interruptions by other people, telephones, doorbells are unlikely;
3. A time when there is no time pressure (for example, not in the 15–20 minutes before an appointment).

We are dealing with a learned skill, not a magic wand. It's hard to develop and maintain this stress reduction skill without regular practice. Now we will practice relaxing.

Relaxation Script

Pause for periods of 5 seconds or more where indicated. Timing of the script is best determined by taping it and then relaxing to the recording.

Make yourself as comfortable as possible, loosen any tight clothing that you can, and get relaxed in your chair. Just focus on your body and feel the tension flow out as you relax more and more. Now, stretch out your legs, lift them slightly off the floor, point your feet back toward your face as much as you can. Tighten your toes, your ankles, your calves, and your thighs—tighten and tighten, as tense as you can. (pause) Now, relax . . . feel the warmth of relaxation in your legs and feet as you relax. Feel how pleasant it is to feel that warmth as it flows through your legs even to your toes. (pause)

Now tighten your buttocks and stomach as hard as you can. Tighten and tighten. Hold it a bit more. (pause) Now, relax . . . buttocks and stomach. Notice the pleasant contrast between the relaxed feeling you experience now and the tightness you experienced a moment ago. Take a deep breath now. As you slowly let it out, also let out the remaining tension in your feet, legs, buttocks, and stomach. Continue to take deep breaths and let them out slowly as we go on. (pause)

Now tighten your back muscles, your chest, and the muscles just under your armpits. Harder. Hold it a little bit longer. (pause) Now relax. Let yourself feel the tranquil flow of relaxation as it moves up your body into your back and chest. Imagine the word *calm* or the word *relax* and think that word to yourself slowly about ten times. Take a deep breath and let it out slowly as the tension drains away. (pause)

Extend your arms and make two fists. Tighten your triceps, your forearms, and your fists. Hard. Really hard. When I say relax, let your arms fall to your lap with the pull of gravity. (pause) Relax. Notice the tingling sensation of relaxation in your fingers and hands. Feel the warmth in your arms. Enjoy this beautiful relaxation. Imagine a peaceful, tranquil scene that is really relaxing. Picture that scene and how warm and comfortable that image is for you. (pause)

Now, hunch up your shoulders as though you are trying to touch them to your ears. Tighten your neck, too. Tighter and tighter. Hold it just a bit more so that your neck actually shakes. (pause) Now, relax. Feel the heaviness in your shoulders and the warm feeling of relaxation. Take a deep breath and slowly let it out. Imagine saying

EXERCISE 14 (cont.)

to yourself, "I am calm and relaxed." Enjoy the comforting feeling of being tension free. (pause)

Now, open your mouth as wide as you can. Wider. Hold it. (pause) Now, relax. Feel the warm, tingling sense in your face. Let your mouth hang open as it relaxes. Breathe deeply. (pause) Now, furrow your brow and tighten your cheek and face muscles into a tight grimace. Tighter. Hold it. (pause) Now, relax. Feel the flow of warm relaxation enter your face and eyes. Enjoy the wonderful feeling of relaxation through your entire body.

Now take a deep breath and hold it. (pause) As you let it out fully, let any tension drain from your whole body. Imagine that your body is being immersed in a warm fluid which absorbs any remaining tension. Feel your body sink into this pleasant fluid little by little and the tension seep from your body. First your feet and legs, then your torso, your arms, your neck, and your head. Breathe deeply and enjoy this relaxed feeling. (pause) I will count to three. On three you will open your eyes and be refreshed and relaxed—one, two, three.

Adapted with permission from P. Jakubowski & A. J. Lange. *The assertive option: Your rights & responsibilities.* Champaign, Ill.: Research Press, 1978.

STRESS SYMPTOMS HANDOUT

PHYSICAL

Increased heart rate
Tightness of chest
Difficulty breathing
Sweaty palms
Trembling, tics, and twitching
Tightness of neck or back
Headache
Urinary frequency, diarrhea
Nausea or vomiting
Constant state of fatigue
Muscular contractions
    (jaws, forehead, neck and
    shoulders, etc.)
Susceptibility to minor illness
Slumped posture

BEHAVIORAL

Procrastination, inability to
    complete projects
Sleep disturbance (increased or
    decreased sleep)
Appetite disturbance (eating
    either more or less)
Increase in smoking or
    drinking
Accident proneness
Avoidance of physical exercise
Restlessness, disturbed
    concentration
Tendency to cry
Decreased involvement with
    others
Math and grammatical errors
Blocking (not hearing)
Decrease in productivity

PSYCHOLOGICAL

Feelings of worthlessness
Depression
Suspiciousness, jealousy
Anxiousness
Cynicism, negativism
Lack of capacity for enjoyment
Decreased initiative
Tendency to blame others
Self-depreciating, self-critical
Forgetfulness, preoccupation
Decreased or increased fantasy
    life
Lack of concentration
Decreased interest
Lack of attention to details
Past oriented, not present
Decreased creativity
Decreased sexual interest
Irritability, angry outbursts
Boredom
Apathy

IRRATIONAL BELIEFS HANDOUT

1. *It is an absolute necessity for an adult to have love and approval from peers, family, and friends.* In fact, it is impossible to please all the people in your life. Even those who basically like and approve of you will be turned off by some behaviors and qualities.

2. *You must be unfailingly competent and almost perfect in all you undertake.* The results of believing you must behave perfectly are self-blame for inevitable failure, lowered self-esteem, perfectionistic standards applied to mate and friends, and paralysis and fear at attempting anything.

3. *Certain people are evil, wicked, and villainous and should be punished.* A more realistic position is that they are behaving in ways that are antisocial or inappropriate. They are perhaps acting stupidly, ignorantly, or neurotically, and it would be well if their behavior could be changed.

4. *It is horrible when people and things are not the way you would like them to be.* This might be described as the spoiled child syndrome. As soon as the tire goes flat, the self-talk starts: "Why does this happen to me? Damn, I can't take this. It's awful. I'll get all filthy." Any inconvenience, problem, or failure to get your way is likely to be met with such awfulizing self-statements.

5. *External events cause most human misery—people simply react as events trigger their emotions.* A logical extension of this belief is that you must control the external events in order to create happiness or avoid sorrow. Since such control has limitations, and we are at a loss to completely manipulate the wills of others, a sense of helplessness and chronic anxiety results.

6. *You should feel fear or anxiety about anything that is unknown, uncertain, or potentially dangerous.* Many people say, "A little bell goes off and I think I ought to start worrying." They begin to rehearse their scenarios of catastrophe. Increasing anxiety in the face of uncertainty makes coping more difficult and adds to stress.

IRRATIONAL BELIEFS HANDOUT (cont.)

7. *It is easier to avoid than to face life's difficulties and responsibilities.* There are many ways of ducking responsibilities: "I'd like to get another job, but I'm just too tired on my days off to look," "A leaky faucet won't hurt anything," "We could shop today, but the car is making a sort of funny sound."

8. *You need something other or stronger or greater than yourself to rely on.* This belief becomes a psychological trap in which your independent judgment and the awareness of your particular needs are undermined by a reliance on higher authority.

9. *The past has a lot to do with determining the present.* Just because you were once strongly affected by something does not mean that you must continue the habits you formed to cope with the original situation. Those old patterns and ways of responding are just decisions made so many times they have become nearly automatic.

10. *You are helpless and have no control over what you experience or feel.* This belief is at the heart of much depression and anxiety. The truth is we not only exercise considerable control over interpersonal situations, we control how we interpret and emotionally respond to each life event.

11. *If you don't go to great lengths to please others, they will abandon or reject you.* This belief is a by-product of low self-esteem. You usually run less risk of rejection if you offer others your true unembellished self. They can take it or leave it. But if they respond to the real you, you don't have to worry about slacking off, letting down your guard, and being rejected later.

12. *When people disapprove of you, it invariably means you are wrong or bad.* This extremely crippling belief sparks chronic anxiety in most interpersonal situations. The irrationality is contained in the generalization of one specific fault or unattractive feature to a total indictment of the self.

IRRATIONAL BELIEFS HANDOUT (cont.)

13. *Happiness, pleasure, and fulfillment can only occur in the presence of others, and being alone is horrible.* Pleasure, self-worth, and fulfillment can be experienced alone as well as with others. Being alone is growth producing and desirable at times.

14. *There is a perfect love and a perfect relationship.* Subscribers to this belief often feel resentful of one close relationship after another. Nothing is quite right because they are waiting for the perfect fit. It never comes.

15. *You shouldn't have to feel pain. You are entitled to a good life.* The realistic position is that pain is an inevitable part of human life. It frequently accompanies tough, healthy decisions and the process of growth. Life is not fair, and sometimes you will suffer no matter what you do.

Adapted with permission from M. Davis, E. R. Eshelman, & M. McKay. *The relaxation and stress reduction workbook.* Richmond, CA: New Harbinger, 1980 and from *REASON & EMOTION IN PSYCHOTHERAPY.* Copyright © 1962 by Dr. Albert Ellis. Published by arrangement with Lyle Stuart.

Chapter Seven

Communication

Abusive couples typically have rather marked deficits in the area of communication. Their evaluation of this state of affairs may be expressed as "We don't communicate at all." By this they may mean that they are more likely to communicate nonverbally than verbally or that they communicate far more negative than positive content.

This deficit in communication skills contributes to the likelihood of additional abusive interactions. Lacking an ability to express themselves clearly and resolve conflict, they are unable to get their needs met through appropriate efforts at social influence. Their ineffective efforts to communicate frequently result in an escalation rather than a resolution of conflict. Learning basic communication principles and practicing communication skills is crucial to alleviating spouse abuse.

COMMUNICATION PRINCIPLES

Understanding the following principles is essential to improving communication.

1. The message sent is not always the message received.
2. It is impossible not to communicate.
3. Every message has content and feeling.
4. Nonverbal cues are more believable than verbal ones.

Message Sent Is Not Always Message Received

People often assume that because they said something, or simply because they thought or intended something ("She knows I don't like it done that way" or "I told her I love her when we got married. She knows it"), that any failure to understand or comply is the fault of the person receiving the message rather than the communication process. When people understand that the message sent is not necessarily the message received, they can begin to clarify their communications rather than automatically cast blame when problems arise. This shift in conceptualizing problems in process rather than personality terms is an extremely important goal.

The message sent (intent) may not be the message received (impact) because the message must pass through what has been called a "filtering process" (Gottman, Notarius, Gonso, & Markman, 1976). What the speaker intends to communicate may not be what he actually expresses when the message passes through his filter of thoughts and feelings. As an example, if the speaker is preoccupied or irritated about something that happened at work, the filter may cause a statement to sound distant or harsh when he responds to his wife. This may occur without intention or even awareness.

The message must pass through the listener's filter where additional distortions may occur. Here, if the listener expects her spouse to be angry, she may hear even positively intended statements as insincere or sarcastic.

The only way to be sure that the message sent is actually the message received is through the process of *feedback*. This is what happens when the speaker asks what impact his communication had on the listener, and the listener provides this information. In the absence of feedback, people generally assume that the message sent is the message received, which may lead them to feel confused and misunderstood. Obviously, there is ample room for misunderstanding between what the speaker intended to say, what was actually said, and what the listener heard.

Exercise 15, Message Sent and Message Received, provides an example of miscommunication for discussion purposes in part A and a role play that focuses on the unspoken intent of spoken messages in part B.

It Is Impossible Not to Communicate

In a relationship there is no such thing as not communicating since all actions have a communication value. When a husband comes home from work and goes directly to the den to watch TV rather than speaking to his family, he is not not communicating. This is actually a powerful, if ambiguous, communication.

It is not possible for people to conceal when they are upset within ongoing relationships, although it may be possible for them to conceal what they are upset about. A wife may naturally assume that her husband is upset with her when he is upset but won't explain why he is.

Since people cannot not communicate, it is best to *put negative content into words*. Both verbal and nonverbal communications work quite well to convey positive messages (a touch, a look, etc.) but non-verbal communications of displeasure can too easily lead to an avoidance of responsibility. The wife who is glaring at her husband can insist that he must be mistaken, nothing is bothering her, and resolution of the issue becomes impossible.

The concept of promptly putting negative content into words must be tempered with a discussion of how to express this content in a manner that is not destructive. Problems only become worse when avoided or expressed nonverbally since displeasure will always be communicated. It's simply a question of whether it will be promptly and constructively expressed verbally or indirectly and irresponsibly expressed nonverbally. This principle is developed in more detail in the section on making requests, page 147.

Part A of Exercise 16, It Is Impossible Not to Communicate, provides a role play in which couples try not to communicate. Part B asks couples to generate a list of their indirect expressions of displeasure.

Every Message Has Content and Feeling

Every message consists of the content, which is the actual information that would be conveyed if the message were to be converted to print, and the feeling component, which is the inflection, gestures, and nonverbal cues used to express the content. The feeling component has also been referred to as "metacommunication" from the Greek word *meta* or *about*. Thus the feeling component is a communication about the communication.

Discrepancies between the content and feeling components of a message can confuse the listener. In "double-bind" communications, the listener cannot comply with both the content and feeling components of a message. For example, the father who smiles (thus conveying approval) while lecturing his son on how bad it was to have hit a friend is putting his son in a double-bind situation.

Exercise 17, Content and Feeling Components, illustrates the importance of inflection in expressing a message in part A and gives clients visual and verbal examples of double-bind communications in part B.

Nonverbal Cues Are More Believable Than Verbal Ones

Whenever there is a discrepancy between the content and the feeling components of a message, the feeling component is given the most weight by the listener (Stuart, 1980b). For example, if a husband were to say to his wife "You sure look great today," the inflection and nonverbal cues could suggest that he, in fact, thought she looked quite good; or, she looked good today as opposed to all those days when she did not look good; or, that he meant just the opposite, that she looked terrible today. Consistency between the two levels of any message is the goal to be strived for to reduce misunderstanding.

Exercise 18, Nonverbal and Verbal Cues, shows how the nonverbal component of a message is given most importance in interpreting a communication.

COMMUNICATION SKILLS

An appreciation of the communication principles prepares couples for the communication skills of listening, validation, feeling-talk, positive expression, negative feeling expression, and request making. The intent is not to make couples into communications experts; rather it is to identify those specific communication skill deficits that contribute most to abusive behavior.

Clients are usually quite interested in the material presented in this section. They have little difficulty in applying the skills to their particular needs and situations and are readily able to see how the failure to employ these skills has led to difficulties in the past. Once again, the positive emphasis on specific techniques that have obvious application in eliminating violence encourages clients' participation and motivation.

Listening

Listening attentively is among the most powerful reinforcers that spouses can provide for each other. It is also a relatively scarce and undervalued occurrence in most troubled relationships. A number of fairly extensive programs to teach listening and empathy skills have been devised (Guerney, 1977; Miller, Wackman, Nunnally, & Saline, 1981). The basic principles about listening that are important for couples in abusive relationships are the importance of listening, the obstacles to listening, the preconditions for listening, and the process or skill of listening.

1. Importance of listening. The importance of listening is evident when we observe what typically occurs between a couple when one partner has something important to say and feels that the message is not being heard. Escalation of the volume and level of rhetoric or sullen withdrawal are common reactions.

Many men who tend to be action oriented underestimate the importance of listening. When their wives complain, they may shift from a listening to a problem-solving mode, and if a solution is not quickly accomplished, they may experience frustration. These men will often report that they have rapidly gone through the following sequence while listening to their wives' complaints: concern and sympathy, a desire to help, then a sense of frustration when a solution is not readily available, which is expressed as anger at the wife ("You shouldn't let people push you around," "You shouldn't be upset," or "I told you what to do about that problem last week"). It can be helpful to teach these couples to signal when they are asking for advice and when they just want to be listened to.

2. Obstacles to listening. Among the most common factors that interfere with the ability to listen, particularly in those relationships where a high level of conflict is the norm, are a lack of interest in what the spouse may have to say, the fear that the listener may be expected to change behavior based on what is said or requested, a desire to maintain a one-up position, or a reluctance to extend the courtesy and respect implied by the act of listening.

Many people confuse listening with complying, and fear that if they seem to listen to a request, complaint, or observation of another, the act of listening will be interpreted as agreement and compliance. Distinguishing between listening, acknowledging the legitimacy of the message, and complying as three separate functions is critical. It is safe to listen, and listening does not cost anything because it does not automatically commit the listener to compliance. It does, however, communicate respect and concern, and as such, can dramatically reduce the likelihood of conflict escalation.

3. Preconditions for listening. The preconditions required for listening include a commitment to listen, physical and mental readiness, and the willingness to let the other person complete a message before interrupting to speak.

The commitment to listen involves deciding to take the time to relax, attend, and convey the commitment to listen by such actions as turning off the TV or putting down the newspaper. It is important for couples to give some thought to when and how to meet these preconditions. Examples of when communication was attempted while the spouse was about to fall asleep, was involved in a TV show, was on the way to work, or had had too much to drink will serve to underscore the importance of these physical and mental preconditions. Finally, the willingness to permit the other to complete his statement before interrupting involves examining listener biases and assumptions. If one partner is convinced that he knows what the other is going to say, or he assumes that the message will be critical, he will have difficulty with this requirement.

4. The process or skill of listening. The capacity to hear is one that most of us are born with, but listening is a much more active process (Miller et al., 1981). To hear is simply to receive and store information, but a good listener is involved in an exchange that includes:

- Observing—physically orienting toward and attending to the speaker;
- Acknowledging—paraphrasing and providing feedback that signals an accurate reception of the message;
- Encouraging—inviting the speaker to continue;
- Checking out—requesting more information in order to reduce confusion; and
- Interpreting—struggling to understand fully.

Exercise 19, Preconditions for Listening, asks couples to think of positive preconditions that would improve their ability to listen and discuss them using listening skills.

Validation

Validation is a skill that is closely related to listening. If listening implies to the wife that her husband cares enough about her and her opinions to make the effort to listen, then validation is the process through which he communicates that her position is considered to be legitimate. The function of validation is to distinguish between people and their behavior or opinions so that they know that even if others do not share their perspective or agree with them, their opinions are still taken seriously. It is a way, then, for a husband to communicate that he assumes that his wife and her opinions are understandable and legitimate even if he does not share them. He is not saying, "You are right and I'm wrong"; he is simply agreeing that her position makes sense given her perspective.

Regardless of how absurd a statement may be, it is still possible to validate it. For example:

Sally: The kids were just terrible today. I'm about at the end of my rope with them and here is what I think we should do. We should put an ad in the paper and sell them to the highest bidder.

George (1):   That's the craziest idea I've ever heard, and you're a terrible human being for ever considering it.

George (2):   Sounds like you're really worn out and fed up with the kids. I could sure see how you could feel that way. But, maybe selling them isn't the best response. Let's figure something out.

In this example, the validity of the wife's feelings were accepted without implying agreement with the proposed solution.

Judy: I've had it with this car. It's driving me crazy not being able to depend on it. I'm going to just push it into a ditch and get a new one.

Dale (1):   You're nuts! You know we can't afford a new car. You don't even make enough to . . .

Dale (2):   It really is a pain. If I'd had as much trouble with it as you have, I'd probably feel the same way. I don't really agree that we can afford a new car right now, but let's look at the figures.

Again, the second response communicates acceptance of the legitimacy of the person and her opinion without also stating agreement. In both examples the spouse was working from the assumption that if he could manage to see it from his partner's point of view, her position, no matter how absurdly stated, would make some sense.

Validation is based on the ability to empathize. The conflict-containment section in Chapter Eight will detail how arguments escalate from dealing with issues ("This car is driving me crazy") to dealing with personalities ("You must be nuts"). The use of validation serves to distinguish between the issue and the personality and, thus, to contain the conflict at an issue level where resolution is possible. Another way of applying this principle to conflict containment is to think of conflict in terms of "different than" rather than in terms of "right and wrong" as in "We see this issue differently" instead of "You are wrong again."

Labeling and perceiving someone as an object facilitates anger, while empathy inhibits it. The empathy-nonaggressive hypothesis (Feshbach, 1964) states quite clearly that anger and violence are inhibited to the extent that a person can empathize with others, and it is through the process of validation that empathy is conveyed.

Exercise 20, Validation, gives couples practice in validating each other's positions.

Feeling-Talk

"He never tells me how he feels." "She never tells me what is bothering her." These statements express the importance couples place on being included in the other's world of experience. Feeling-talk or self-expression is simply the skill of informing people clearly and directly about inner feelings. By putting emotions into words, both the speaker and the listener become clearer about what's going on, and prompt expression of negative feelings serves to keep pressure from building.

Often there are certain beliefs or catastrophic expectations (Gottman et al., 1976) that get in the way of the expression of feelings: "I will seem weak if I say it out loud," "My partner will be devastated," "I will lose control of myself," "The relationship will be hurt beyond repair."

Men may hold many of these beliefs that make it difficult for them to engage in feeling-talk because of how they were socialized to view the expression of feelings. Before learning to engage in feeling-talk, couples need to understand why this type of exchange can be so difficult, particularly for men.

In the vast majority of relationships where companionship has become an issue, it is the female who feels the need for a greater degree of intimacy, self-disclosure, and feeling-talk. Males typically find it difficult to meet this need, and frequently because they do not share their wives' high evaluation of feeling-talk, they are somewhat confused by the importance their wives place on this activity.

Parents teach their children how to be either a man or woman. In our culture to be masculine is to express aggressiveness, toughness, competitiveness, independence, and courage. Parents who describe their son proudly as being "all boy" are probably commenting on the fact that he is adventurous, athletic, rough, and inclined to like to climb trees and get dirty. If he were to cry or express sentimental or soft emotions, he would most likely be admonished that big boys don't do that sort of thing. The message is clear that expressing certain emotions is feminine and, above all else, to be masculine is to avoid being feminine. Until very recently, men were generally socialized to believe that anger was acceptable, but that they should not express tenderness, concern, or anything that might sound weak. This is still a prevailing ethic in many settings ("Anything wrong, soldier?" "No, *sir*"). Women, on the other hand, learned that the direct expression of angry feelings was unladylike.

Balswick and Peek in their article "The Inexpressive Male: A Tragedy of American Society" (1971) suggest that two basic models of inexpressive behavior result from this socialization process: the cowboy (John Wayne) type and the playboy (James Bond) type. The cowboy avoids any displays of tenderness or affection. He is somewhat uncomfortable around women, treating them in a distant, man-to-man fashion with just a hint of tenderness. His horse, however, is always ready right outside, to ride off into the sunset and back to more important business. He is courteous but reserved around women, and seems to value his girlfriend and his horse equally. The cowboy, then, cares for women but is careful not to let it show as that would be inconsistent with the image.

The playboy type also relates to women in a reserved, detached manner, but here the emphasis is on being "cool" and manipulating them to his own ends. He is skillful in knowing what music to play, what food to order, and what drinks to mix, but is careful to avoid anything but a sexual or manipulative involvement. He also differs from the cowboy in that he seems to be not only emotionally remote but somewhat dead emotionally.

Thus, the inexpressive male in our culture is presented with two role models: the inexpressive male with feelings (the cowboy), and the inexpressive male without feelings (the playboy). When the inexpressive male marries, he is almost certain to value companionship and feeling-talk less than his wife, who has been socialized to be more verbal, expressive, warm, and interested in relating in an intimate manner. This is particularly true among the less educated and lower socio-economic groups (who tend to be overrepresented in abusive populations), who are more likely to equate expressiveness with being nonmasculine.

In addition to the almost inevitable conflict over intimacy and the expression of feelings, other consequences of the different early socialization processes experienced by males and females are suggested by Herb Goldberg in his book *The Hazards of Being Male* (1976). Because males are rewarded for being independent, achieving, and task oriented, they are poorly equipped to step easily into the role of husband and father. For females who have learned to value domestic skills and exclusive intimate relationships, the transition to marriage is not as difficult.

As a consequence, the male is programmed to fall short in his efforts as a mature marriage partner. He is faced with the challenge of forcing himself to adopt a role that is dramatically at odds with his early training and is destined to disappoint both himself and his spouse. The result is a chronic sense of guilt and selfishness over his natural, but now unacceptable, impulses. His wife is placed in the role of "permission giver" as he can no longer trust his own judgments and taste. He reacts like a child when caught doing something wrong and may become more and more childish and helpless in his interactions with his wife. She is now a mother figure and he is the child. Wives often describe this transformation by describing their husbands as just like a baby, unable to make decisions, sneaky, and childish.

The guilt leads to resentment and anger which is suppressed. A sense of rage, which the husband is afraid to express directly, may take the form of numerous passive/aggressive acts that result in detachment and alienation from the marriage. Moodiness, retreat into work or drink, having to be reminded to perform small chores, resistance to talking or sharing, avoidance of eye contact with the wife, and a sense of boredom are all suggestive of this condition. Another response is to deny what he would like to do or to fail to express how he really feels. He may stay home to avoid feeling guilty; but because he resents having to do this, he makes himself unavailable to his family while at home.

Unable to express himself or even to accept his own nature, he exercises control over himself by denying his feelings. This makes him vulnerable to sudden outbursts of unpredictable behavior. Temper tantrums over relatively minor irritations, drinking bouts, and expressions of rage and violence are possible consequences. These compound the problem by creating more remorse and self-loathing, and by driving away the family that he would in fact like to, but somehow cannot, be close to.

Exercise 21, Socialization, can prompt discussion of how males and females are socialized differently. By discovering that certain behaviors are the natural but changeable outcome of certain socialization patterns, the tendency to feel unique or to personalize those experiences is reduced.

When they understand why engaging in feeling-talk may be difficult for them, clients may begin to learn how to express their feelings more constructively through feeling-talk. In order to engage in feeling-talk, the speaker must first be able to get in touch with what he is feeling, then articulate the feelings by putting them into words, edit the words in such a way that they can be heard by his spouse, and finally, the spouse must hear and validate the experience in order for it to be likely to be repeated.

Sometimes there is some confusion in differentiating feelings from thoughts or ideas. One simple way of doing this is to state the feeling followed by the word *that*. If it can be expressed after *that*, it is probably an idea rather than an emotion.

"I feel *that* you don't want me around." (idea)

"I feel rejected." (feeling)

"I feel *that* you don't do enough work around here." (idea)

"I feel irritated." (feeling)

Feeling-talk is not a license for total candor. It is important for clients to realize that simply prefacing remarks with "I feel . . ." does not reduce the destructive potential of fully uncensored communication. There is considerable support for the conclusion that distressed couples engage in a much higher frequency of expression of negative statements than do nondistressed couples. Richard Stuart's (1980b) suggestion that couples be advised to follow the "norm of measured honesty" as opposed to the "let-it-all-hang-out" ethic is particularly relevant for this population. There are probably few relationships that could withstand the effects of total honesty.

With this reservation in mind, there are several points that should be followed in making feeling statements.

1. They should be phrased as "I" statements. Statements that begin with *you* almost always sound like an accusation and run the risk of creating defensiveness. Those that begin with *it, we, others, some people* tend to leave the ownership of the feelings unclear and permit the avoidance of the assumption of personal responsibility.

2. They should be in the form of statements rather than questions. Questions are often an indirect way of making a point or an accusation and are rarely taken as simple requests for information. If questions are required, "how" questions are preferable to "why" questions as they are less accusatory.

3. They should be present oriented and promptly stated. For example, "I feel angry," is better than, "It used to upset me when . . . ," which may leave the listener unsure of how things stand now.

4. They should follow the "say-ask" principle. Stuart (1980b) suggests that couples follow the say-ask principle to increase the level of responsibility in discussions. A husband stating his preference before asking his wife for hers, as in "I would like to go out for dinner. What would you like?" is an example of this approach.

Feeling-talk, then, that involves "I" language, statements rather than questions, a present orientation, and follows the "say-ask" principle can have a facilitating influence on the relationship and reduce the buildup of negative emotions and interpersonal conflict. Like most communication skills, it requires considerable practice.

Exercise 22, Getting to Know Your Feelings, uses the Feelings List Handout to help clients identify feelings in part A and asks them to keep a log of their feelings in part B. Exercise 23, Feeling-talk, asks clients to practice feeling-talk.

Positive Expression

Couples involved in domestic violence often appear to be either "burnt-out," treating each other in a cool, impersonal manner, or else in a constant state of conflict, frequently expressing criticism and defensiveness. In either case, the expression of positive, reinforcing statements has typically dropped to a very low level. The observation that marriage partners generally treat strangers with more courtesy than they treat each other tends to be particularly true for abusive couples. They are much more likely to criticize, interrupt, and fail to express appreciation to each other than they would be with others.

Some of the reasons that abusive couples do not engage in positive expression include:

1. They believe that it would be insincere to say something that they do not feel. Here the assumption is made that feeling change has to precede behavioral change, and that feelings will change automatically or in the absence of any effort to bring the change about. People with this belief often follow the "change-second" principle (Stuart, 1980b) in that they will change only after their spouses do. It is easy to see that this causes a standoff that perpetuates the status quo.

2. They underestimate the reinforcing properties of positive statements. They may believe that even though they have positive feelings, there is no reason to express these feelings because their spouses know how they feel. Or, they might think that expressions of appreciation are unnecessary because to act right is just to do your job. These couples don't realize that positive statements can influence their spouses to feel better and to treat them better, which in turn can make them feel better.

3. They lack practice and feel awkward making positive statements. This is very common among abusive couples and is probably related to factors experienced during childhood where criticism may have been much more frequent than praise. Role playing expressing positive statements can be a surprisingly effective means of desensitizing this embarrassment.

The various factors contributing to the low frequency of positive expression can be discussed by asking each client what gets in the way of his making more such statements to his spouse. It is likely that the responses will be similar to those listed. However, regardless of the cause of the low frequency, it is much more important to engage in positive rehearsal than to discuss the past. Each client should be encouraged to experiment with increasing positive expressions, noting both his own feelings and the response of his spouse. The therapist should model the expression of positive feelings by rewarding and complimenting clients liberally. The therapist can also prompt positive expressions by consistently asking clients how they communicated their appreciation when they mention positive efforts made by their spouse.

There are three general categories of positive expressions:

1. Affection and caring. It has been suggested that small, high-frequency expressions of caring are more important than larger events in creating a climate of commitment and marital satisfaction (Stuart, 1980b). Stuart has used the simile that engaging in these caring behaviors is like putting money in the bank, which can be drawn against when difficulties arise. For example, the husband who has kissed his wife goodbye and given her a compliment before leaving for work is likely to get a different response if he returns home an hour late than is the husband who has not engaged in these small positive behaviors.

2. Praise and compliments. The relatively high frequency of negative criticism as opposed to expressions of praise can lead to a feeling of not being appreciated that, in turn, can lead to a reduced effort to relate in a positive manner. When couples begin to exchange compliments, they should be advised to avoid the temptation to include "hooks" ("She's a great cook, when she gets around to it") that negate the compliment's positive value.

3. Expression of appreciation. The "but-what-have-you-done-for-me-lately?" approach is much more common between spouses than between friends. Here, when positive behaviors are engaged in by one partner, the response is simply another request, rather than an expression of thanks. For example, the wife may say to her husband who has just mowed the lawn that their car also needs to be washed.

Exercise 24, Positive Expression, has couples practice positive exchanges in part A using the Positive Expressions Handout, and create a list of caring behaviors and perform them in Part B.

Negative Feeling Expression

The expression of negative feelings needs to be approached with some degree of caution because most couples who have experienced episodes of violence are sensitive to the destructive potential of these emotions.

They tend to either overinhibit or underinhibit the expression of negative feelings as if there were just two modes of conduct in this area—silence or absolute candor.

Clients may have considerable practice in concealing feelings even from themselves and therefore may have found themselves acting in ways that they could not fully understand. They need to accept ambivalent feelings, the coexistence of love and hate, as normal. Appropriate expressions of emotions can be modeled for clients and the range of acceptable behaviors for them expanded. It is important to validate their feelings while helping them find alternative ways of expressing them, always making the distinction between their feelings and their actions.

It is absolutely essential that couples develop the skill of expressing negative feelings and identifying areas of conflict, as both are experienced often in marriage. Couples should be reminded of the impossibility of not communicating. Thus, the choice is simply to express negative content directly, so that issues can be identified and resolved, or indirectly, which leads to confusion, misunderstanding, and withdrawal. Once couples have accepted that negative feelings are to be expected (that is, they are normal), that they cannot be concealed, and that direct expression in words is preferable to indirect (nonverbal) expression, the following additional points should be presented.

First, it is better to express negative feelings promptly. The longer the expression of negative feelings is delayed, the more likely it is that those feelings will be magnified through anger-inducing self-talk. They are also likely to be associated with other unresolved negative feelings, and all of these bad feelings may be dumped on the spouse at one time in an angry explosion. Additionally, the more time that has elapsed since the original negative incident, the more likely it is that the spouse will have a sense of being "ambushed" and think "How long has he felt this way?" or "What can I do about this now?"

Second, the expression of negative feelings must focus on the spouse's behavior and not on personality or essence. For example, it is better for a client to say to his spouse "That was a dumb thing to do," rather than "You are dumb for doing that."

Third, negative feeling expression should take the form of "feeling-cause" statements (Jacobson & Margolin, 1979). These statements involve saying "I feel . . . because . . . " as in "I feel angry because you didn't balance the checkbook." The object is for the couple to learn to inform each other about negative feelings and areas of conflict in such a way that corrective action can be taken. Both the feeling and the behavior that contributed to the feeling should be expressed promptly in feeling-cause statements that focus on the behavior and not the personality and that clearly inform, or at least imply, what action in the future would resolve the conflict. Threats, put-downs, demands, and the use of numerous examples should be avoided by the couple. Clients can role play negative-feeling expression situations, initially selecting issues that have not been conflicts for them so that they can focus on the process of expressing feelings and not the content.

Request Making

One of the most important communication transactions to occur within the marital relationship is that of *request making*. The significance of this act is due in part to the following considerations:

1. It is a high frequency occurrence, with couples typically making numerous requests of each other every day.
2. The way a request is expressed tends to define the relationship in terms of power and authority.
3. How the request is expressed may be more important in determining the listener's response than the content of the request itself.

"Take out the garbage!" "Why don't you ever take out the garbage?" "I would appreciate it if you would take out the garbage." In these three examples, the behavior requested of the listener is identical, but the responses and the feelings elicited by the requests were probably quite different.

Each request, like every message, is composed of two parts, the content and the feeling components. The *content* conveys what is being requested. This is by far the simpler of the two components. Generally, difficulty only arises at this level if the content, or what is being asked of the listener, is unclear or inconsistent with some previous message. In the case of the request to take out the garbage, the listener might not be sure of what garbage or where to take it, or this request might be inconsistent with a previous communication, such as the person who washes the dishes won't be required to also take out the garbage. In either case, questions at the content level are easily cleared up by simply asking for additional information.

The second component of the request, the *feeling component,* has to do with how the request is worded and expressed. Both verbal and nonverbal (inflection, tone of voice, volume, etc.) factors require consideration. It is at this level that most of the difficulties occur, for it is possible to ask the listener to perform the identical act (the content) in a way that may elicit either cooperation, reluctant compliance, or noncompliance.

Each request tends to convey information about how the sender defines his relationship with the receiver. To phrase the request as a command is to imply that the relationship is defined in authoritarian terms with the sender in a position of authority over the receiver. If such a command were complied with by the receiver, it would imply that this definition of the relationship was acceptable. If the receiver does not agree with the authoritarian definition of the relationship, the request might be refused or complied with reluctantly even though the content of the request itself seemed perfectly acceptable.

It is possible for the listener to experience resistance or even anger when receiving such a message without being fully aware of the cause of the ill feelings. Couples will often find themselves arguing about the content of a request when what is really at issue is this relationship component.

Men who work in an environment where directives are frequently communicated as orders may tend to employ the same form of request making in the home without considering the relationship aspects of their communications.

The following guidelines are helpful for couples making positive requests:

- Be prompt.
- Be positive.
- Be specific.
- Use "I" language, *not* "you" language.
- Ask "how" or "what" questions, *not* "why" questions.
- Look for and reward positive compliance.

1. Be prompt. It is best to make requests when they first become an issue rather than silently holding them inside; otherwise, there is the possibility that irritation will build because the listener has not somehow anticipated and complied with the unstated request. There is also the risk of "dumping" several requests at one time. It is preferable to make requests singly and to request only that which the listener is capable of complying with. "Why don't you grow up?" or "I wish you would be more considerate" are not examples of positive requests.

2. Be positive. Requests should be made positively, expressing what is wanted of the listener, not what is not wanted. "Stop making such a mess," "Don't be late," "Don't run all the gas out of the car" are examples of negative requests. The intent is to be descriptive rather than evaluative.

3. Be specific. "I would appreciate it if you would pick up your clothes," "Please be in by 10 o'clock," "I would appreciate it if you would leave at least half a tank of gas, since we want to get an early start tomorrow" are examples of positive and specific requests. "Don't be such a slob" does not convey the information required for compliance even if the listener wanted to.

4. Use "I" language. Requests that begin with *you* almost always sound like accusations and are likely to elicit responses of defensiveness. "You always come in late" will most likely lead to a debate about "always" or about "late" or about who is more guilty of coming in late (all defensive responses) but is unlikely to result in positive compliance. By beginning the request with *I* the speaker assumes responsibility for the request, avoiding any quality of accusation and reducing the listener's need to be defensive.

5. Use "how" or "what," not "why" questions. If questions are required for clarification, *how* or *what* will focus on the process, whereas *why* leads to accusations and defensiveness. "Why didn't you clean up the bathroom?" simply invites excuses when what the speaker is really interested in is the process of getting the room clean. "How will we get it done?" or even "What can I do to help?" are more likely to lead to the desired behavior.

6. Look for and reward positive compliance. Looking for and rewarding positive compliance is probably the most important step in the process. Rewarding positive behavior is much more likely to lead to repetition of the behavior in the future than is any amount of threat or punishment. The effectiveness of positive reinforcement is well recognized, but easily overlooked. If the listener has only partially complied, rewarding what has been done and then pointing out what remains is most likely to lead to successful completion. For example, "The bathtub looks great. Now, the sink needs to be cleaned." People always perform better for the carrot than for the stick.

Exercise 25, Request Making, provides practice in making positive requests according to the six guidelines for making positive requests in part A, uses the Positive Expressions Handout to help men practice giving rewarding statements in part B, and offers a role play to show the difference between imparting information and requesting permission in part C. Exercise 26, Practicing and Evaluating Communication, has clients use the Communication Prompting and Evaluating Worksheet to grade themselves on their use of communication skills in part A, role play how not to communicate in part B, and role play how to communicate in part C.

EXERCISE 15

MESSAGE SENT AND MESSAGE RECEIVED

A. An area in which miscommunication is likely is the area of extend-
ing sexual overtures. In an attempt to avoid embarrassment and
overt rejection, sexual advances are often made in a very indirect
manner. If they are not reciprocated, rejection is assumed. Feedback or clarification is rarely requested, as it is assumed that the
message sent was the message received. For example, the wife may
express her sense of hurt that the husband did not make love to her
because he "knows" that when she takes a shower at night she is
feeling particularly sexy. Ask couples to share the signals they
might exchange in this situation, and any examples of miscommunication that they can recall.

B. The following example (Gottman et al., 1976) can be role played
to demonstrate that the message sent is not always the message
received.

HUSBAND Unspoken Intent or Impact (He thinks)	Spoken Message	Spoken Message	WIFE Unspoken Intent or Impact (She thinks)
She's got a new sweater. I wonder if it is new. She looks good in it.	Is that a new sweater?		
		I got it on sale!	He thinks I'm a spendthrift!
Boy, is she nasty. Well, I have been denying my- self a new pipe, sticking to our budget.	Where did you buy it?		

HUSBAND Unspoken Intent (He thinks)	Spoken Message	Spoken Message	WIFE Unspoken Intent (She thinks)
		None of your business!	I'm not putting up with this third-degree police investigation.
I'll show her.	I'm going to buy a new pipe. I'll show you whose business it is!		
		I don't care what you do.	He certainly is childish.

Adapted with permission from J. Gottman, C. Notarius, J. Gonso, & H. Markham. *A couple's guide to communication*. Champaign, Ill.: Research Press, 1976.

EXERCISE 16

IT IS IMPOSSIBLE NOT TO COMMUNICATE

A. Ask a couple to role play the following situation:
   Wife—You are to convince your husband to do something with you that you very much want to do. It may be visit your family, make a large purchase, go on vacation. Be persistent.
   Husband—As your wife attempts to convince you to do something, you are to attempt to not communicate in any way.

B. Ask participants to discuss with their partners how they can tell when each is upset by something. It should be possible to generate a list of indirect expressions of displeasure. Then ask the recipients of this information if the descriptions fit; that is, are those accurate statements of how they occasionally express negative emotions. In this way they will assume ownership of these behaviors, acknowledge their intent or communication value, and may thereby make these less available for future conflicts. Example:

EXERCISE 16 (cont.)

HUSBAND TENDS TO:	WIFE TENDS TO:
Clench jaw muscles	Act very busy
Scowl	Whistle
Drive fast	Insist that nothing is wrong
Complain that the house is a mess	Take it out on the kids
	Pout
Insist that *nothing* is wrong	Act hurt
Watch TV until late at night	Roll up in a ball on her side of the bed
Withdraw from family activities	

EXERCISE 17

CONTENT AND FEELING COMPONENTS

A. The importance of inflection in qualifying the content of a message can be suggested by writing the following sentence:

"I never said you spoiled our son."

Read this sentence seven times, placing the emphasis on a different word with each reading. The meaning conveyed is quite different with each inflection.

I never said—but others did.
I *never* said—I wouldn't be so stupid as to say it.
I never *said*—I may have thought it.
you spoiled our son—maybe your parents, but not you.
spoiled—you have damaged him in some other way.
our—maybe your son.
son—now our daughter, maybe.

B. The idea that there can be an inconsistency between the content and the context (feeling component) of a message can be visually represented with the following examples of double-bind communications.

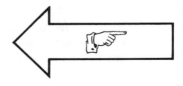

Present these visual examples and the following verbal examples of double-bind communications to clients and ask them to discuss any that they can recall experiencing and the sense of confusion that resulted.

1. The father who smiles (thus conveying approval) while lecturing his son on how bad it was to have punched a friend.
2. The wife who complains that her husband never says he loves her, but who responds when he says it by saying that he is only doing it because she asked and therefore it's not genuine. Or the confusion that can occur when a wife says, "I don't want you just to make love to me, I want you to want to make love." These examples suggest the dilemma of doing something upon request that is by definition spontaneous.
3. The wife who tells her husband who has called asking if she minds if he goes out drinking with the boys, "*Sure,* go right ahead and leave me alone with the kids for a couple more hours." He senses her disapproval and comes home rather than going out only to be met with "I never said you couldn't go out drinking."

EXERCISE 18

NONVERBAL AND VERBAL CUES

Ask couples to turn to each other and deliver a compliment in a sarcastic tone; for example, "You sure look *great* today" or "I can see that you are really sticking to that diet." Then, ask whether they responded to the content (words) or to the feeling component.

EXERCISE 19

PRECONDITIONS FOR LISTENING

Ask each couple to consider the information just covered on listening. Ask each spouse to work independently and think of several positive preconditions that would improve his ability to communicate. They should discuss these preconditions, practicing observing, acknowledging, encouraging, checking out, and interpreting.

EXERCISE 19 (cont.)

A simple technique for couples to employ if they find that they are interrupting each other is to select an object, such as a pencil, and agree that the person holding the object has the floor. A person can only speak when he has the object and must wait until he has the object before responding.

EXERCISE 20

VALIDATION

Ask each spouse to express a position and have the other respond in a way that validates the position without necessarily agreeing or complying. The use of exaggerated or preposterous positions can test the ability to validate and introduce an element of humor.

EXERCISE 21

SOCIALIZATION

Discuss the following issues related to how males and females are socialized differently.

1. Is the description of the socialization of males and females consistent with what clients experienced while growing up?
2. Is the observation that females require and participate more in open expressions of intimacy true of their relationship?
3. If the model fits, what are the implications for their marriage? How can they begin to compromise on how much time should be spent together, apart, and in feeling-talk?
4. Do the men ever feel like little boys in relating to their wives, and do the wives ever feel like permission givers?
5. When people become aware of the effects of socialization, are there things that they can do to change or offset this influence?

EXERCISE 22

GETTING TO KNOW YOUR FEELINGS

A. It takes practice to become aware of feelings and to be able to put them into words. Distribute the Feelings List Handout and ask clients to review it several times a day over the next week. Each time they do, they should pick the word or words that best describe their feelings. They should then spend a minute or so considering exactly what makes up that particular feeling, what parts of the body are affected, and what the signals are that this is the emotion that is being experienced.

A variation is to ask clients to go through the list and think of times when they have experienced each of the emotions listed. Again, the purpose is to help them get in touch with their feelings and to communicate acceptance of the idea that it is all right to experience a range of feelings.

B. Request that clients keep a record of their different feelings or emotions as they become aware of experiencing them during the coming week. For each feeling, ask them to detail the accompanying sensations to assist them in detecting and labeling various states of arousal.

EXERCISE 23

FEELING-TALK

Once they have acquired the ability to detect and label feelings, clients are ready to practice feeling-talk. Their feeling-talk should:

1. Be phrased as "I" statements,
2. Use statements rather than questions,
3. Be present oriented and promptly stated,
4. Follow the "say-ask" principle.

Ask each client to engage in feeling-talk at least one time per day during the week and to report his success at the next session.

EXERCISE 24

POSITIVE EXPRESSION

A. For this exercise, ask clients to read over the Positive Expression Handout. Asking clients to read this aloud often elicits manifestations of discomfort of surprising proportions, and can lead to a discussion of why this is so difficult. After reviewing the list, ask couples to experiment by expressing positive statements at least three times a day during the next week. Anticipate resistance by instructing that you would like them to do it even though it may feel phony or "not real."

B. Ask the couples to make a list of at least twelve small, high-frequency behaviors that they could exchange that would communicate caring. Examples might include: giving a compliment, asking about the spouse's day, helping with a chore, expressing appreciation, touching. Then ask them to agree to do at least two of these each day over the coming week.

   Again, state that you are asking them to do this as an experiment and that they are to do it in spite of any feelings of awkwardness. Discuss the importance of changing behavior in order to change feelings rather than waiting for feelings to somehow change first.

EXERCISE 25

REQUEST MAKING

A. Generate a list of problematic requests and ask couples to role play negative examples of making each request and then positive examples, using the guidelines for making positive requests. (Be prompt. Be positive. Be specific. Use "I" language. Use "how" or "what," not "why" questions. Look for and reward positive compliance.) The guidelines should be thoroughly understood before beginning the role play.

B. Have the husbands practice giving positive rewarding statements. Use the Positive Expressions Handout to act as a prompt. Repeat until they are desensitized to any awkwardness. This exercise may lead to a discussion of duty: "Why should I reward someone for just doing her job?" "Nobody ever tells me when I do something right."

C. Ask the husbands to role play some variations of how they would inform their wives of the following situation: You have just been told by your boss that you are to leave in 1 week for a 4-day business trip. You are aware that your wife had some plans for the family during this time. This role play often leads to discussions about whether the husband is imparting information or requesting the wife's permission. Encourage the husbands to follow these steps:

   1. Promptly and completely present the information.
   2. Actively listen to the wife's response and communicate that listening is occurring.
   3. Find something to agree with: "Yes, I can see how you would be disappointed. It's upsetting to me, too."
   4. If necessary, restate the facts of the situation: "However, it will be necessary for us to comply."

EXERCISE 26

PRACTICING AND EVALUATING COMMUNICATION

A. Distribute the Communication Prompting and Evaluating Worksheet and ask each client to grade himself on his use of the various communication skills for the week. The purpose is to help clients recall the various points made in the communications lecture and to prompt positive behavioral rehearsal.

EXERCISE 26 (cont.)

B. The same worksheet can be distributed and couples asked to have a brief discussion on a trivial, rather than a highly charged, conflict area. Ask that they make as many communication errors as possible as they do it. Possible topics would be what to have for dinner, what TV show to watch, or who should get new license plates for the car. Points are earned for not listening, interrupting, failing to acknowledge, and other errors. The worksheet checklist can be completed to see if they managed to be truly lousy communicators.

C. The above exercise can then be repeated with instructions to do as many things right as possible. Again, the worksheet can serve as a prompt for positive communication and a way to evaluate performance.

FEELINGS LIST HANDOUT

accepted	feminine	lovable	self-reliant
affectionate	flirtatious	loving	sexy
afraid	friendly	loyal	shy
angry	frustrated	manipulated	silly
appreciated	generous	masculine	sinful
attractive	grateful	misunderstood	soft
awkward	guilty	needy	sorry
beautiful	happy	old	stubborn
brave	hateful	optimistic	stupid
calm	hopeful	passionate	superior
comfortable	hopeless	peaceful	supportive
competent	hostile	persecuted	suspicious
concerned	humorous	pessimistic	sympathetic
confident	hurt	phony	tender
confused	ignored	playful	terrified
content	impatient	pleased	threatened
curious	inadequate	possessive	touchy
defeated	incompetent	prejudiced	unappreciated
dejected	indecisive	preoccupied	uncertain
dependent	independent	pressured	understanding
depressed	inferior	protective	uptight
desperate	inhibited	proud	used
disappointed	insecure	quiet	useless
eager	insincere	rejected	victimized
easygoing	involved	remorseful	violent
embarrassed	isolated	sad	weary
envious	jealous	secure	wishy-washy
excited	lonely	seductive	youthful

POSITIVE EXPRESSIONS HANDOUT

AFFECTION AND CARING

"I like you."
"You are easy to like."
"I enjoy being with you."
"I was really concerned about you."
"I missed you."
"I love you."
"I really care about you."
"We make a pretty good team."

PRAISE AND COMPLIMENTS

"That's great!"
"You really look good."
"You are doing fine."
"Good idea."
"That was a great meal."
"It was really fun to be with you."
"I have faith in you."
"I can't think of anybody I'd rather be with."

APPRECIATION

"Thanks."
"I really appreciate that."
"You sure were helpful."
"I can see that you put a lot of effort into that."
"That was very thoughtful."
"You did a great job."
"I couldn't have done it without you."
"Things would be a lot harder if it weren't for you."

COMMUNICATION PROMPTING
AND EVALUATING WORKSHEET

Use the following score sheet to evaluate your effectiveness as a communicator, keeping the following communication principles in mind.

1. The message sent is not always the message received.
2. It is impossible not to communicate.
3. Every message has content and feeling.
4. Nonverbal cues are more believable than verbal ones.

SKILLS	Not so good 1	2	3	4	Good 5
LISTENING					
Commitment to listen					
Physical and mental readiness					
Not interrupting					
Observing					
Acknowledging					
Encouraging					
Checking out					
Interpreting					
VALIDATION					
Issues not personalities					
FEELING-TALK					
Measured honesty					
"I" not "you" language					
Statements not questions					
Present oriented					
Say-ask principle					

COMMUNICATION PROMPTING
AND EVALUATING WORKSHEET (cont.)

SKILLS	Not so good 1	2	3	4	Good 5
POSITIVE EXPRESSION					
Affection and caring					
Praise and compliments					
Expression of appreciation					
NEGATIVE FEELING EXPRESSION					
Prompt					
Behavior not personality					
Feeling-cause statements					
REQUEST MAKING					
Prompt					
Positive					
Specific					
"I" not "you" language					
"How" or "what" not "why" questions					
Rewarding positive compliance					

Chapter Eight

The Inevitability of Conflict

Couples who do not practice effective communication and nonviolent problem-solving skills are likely to resort to manipulative, coercive, maladaptive, and perhaps violent, techniques to achieve what they perceive to be an equitable balance in the relationship. When withdrawal or more overt forms of punishment are used by one spouse, they almost always elicit more punishing behaviors on the part of the other spouse and the process of conflict escalation is initiated. The following example of conflict escalation that resulted in physical violence is taken from Bagarozzi and Giddings (1982). The conflict began because Mrs. Smith wanted her husband to be more affectionate and believed he was only affectionate when he wanted to have intercourse.

> In order to punish him, Mrs. Smith refuses to have sex with her husband. Mr. Smith reciprocates the punishment by verbally abusing his wife and calling her "frigid." She escalates the coercion by attacking Mr. Smith's masculinity and sexual performance. After several months of such arguments, Mr. Smith loses his temper and strikes his wife. His striking his wife has immediate instrumental consequences, because it terminates Mrs. Smith's verbal attacks. After a few days of emotional divorce, Mr. Smith's guilt forces him to apologize to his wife. He becomes attentive and affectionate, and after a week or so of his increased attention, Mrs. Smith forgives him. Mr. and Mrs. Smith make up by having sexual relations. (p. 326)

In this example, it is apparent that the couple resorted to a variety of coercive tactics in order to get their needs met. Mrs. Smith discovered that she could elicit affection from her husband by provoking guilt, and Mr. Smith learned that the use of violence will cause his wife to cease her verbal attacks. Here the violence cycle can be thought of as gradually escalating over several months. It is likely to be repeated because the use of violence was reinforced, and because the couple was, in all probability, unaware of the cycle and how each participated in it and perpetuated it.

The vast majority of expressive violence is experienced by clients in the context of escalating conflict. In order for them to be successful in eliminating violence, they must learn to contain conflict, and learn and employ constructive, noncoercive problem-solving and conflict-resolution skills. To develop the required skills, it is necessary for them to realize that conflict is a fact of life in relationships. It will be helpful for them to identify any unrealistic attitudes or beliefs that may make it difficult for them to recognize the need for conflict-containment skills.

Couples who experience difficulty with anger and violence often subscribe to certain beliefs or maintain certain expectations concerning their relationship that contribute to the problem. The idea that relationships should at all times be harmonious and soothing and that it is drastically wrong if they are not can lead to the inhibition of feelings or avoidance of dealing with problems while they are still at a manageable level. The belief that one's will must prevail, that there must be total agreement between spouses on all issues, or that a conflict must be resolved once and for all before harmony can be restored can keep couples arguing long past the point of any benefit. The perception that they alone are experiencing conflict or that other families seem to get along much better can heighten the perceived need for conflict resolution. And, finally, the expectations that they are entitled to have all their needs met, that they shouldn't have to negotiate, that their spouses can read their minds, or that love should conquer all detract from a willingness to master and employ communication and conflict-containment skills.

In this chapter, the potential sources of conflict and the issues over which couples commonly experience conflict are covered in order to normalize the issue of conflict. Several approaches to conflict resolution are presented to increase clients' awareness of the range of responses available to them when conflict does occur and to provide them with a nomenclature for identifying their own approach to conflict resolution. Constructive problem-solving and negotiation skills are presented and contrasted with destructive approaches to conflict.

SOURCES OF FAMILY CONFLICT

Reviewing many of the potential sources of intrafamily conflict experienced by the majority of couples (Gelles & Straus, 1979) will help couples realize that it is not realistic to expect to achieve a conflict-free marriage. These sources of family stress and conflict are faced by all families, not just by troubled families. What is critical for clients is to recognize the issues and learn to deal with them constructively. Clients need to develop a tolerance for conflict and accept and contain disagreement rather than attempting to eliminate it. They should not expect to agree on all or even most issues.

1. Time. The most basic factor accounting for conflict is simply the amount of time spent together and the enforced closeness experienced by family members. In other relationships, conflicts can be escaped, avoided, or disregarded much more easily.

2. Range of activities. The family must engage in a wide range of activities and master a range of mutual tasks that far exceeds what is expected of other more narrowly focused groupings.

3. Intensity of interests. The topics that the family must contend with and reach agreement on are quite important (financial priorities, moral decisions, child rearing, etc.).

4. Right to influence. Family members feel the right to express interest and influence over the conduct of each other. When those other than family are involved, an opinion might be held, but probably not freely expressed.

5. Age and sex. The family is composed of members of different gender and age, thus setting the stage for both "battle of the sexes" and "generation gaps."

6. Privacy. Family conflicts occur in the privacy of the home and away from the moderating influence of others.

7. Involuntary membership. The fact that the relationships are viewed as exclusive and permanent ones eliminates the option for members of conflict resolution through leaving the group or submitting a resignation.

8. High stress level. The stress imposed by various developmental changes such as birth, aging, and retirement makes the nuclear family inherently unstable.

9. Approval of violence. The acceptance of violence between siblings, and between parent and child in the form of punishment, also contributes to the level of conflict.

In addition to a familiarity with the sources of conflict, knowledge about the types of issues couples experience conflict over also serves a normalizing function. According to Stuart (1980b), during the first year of marriage, the topics that are the focus for most arguments are sex, money, and how the partner acts. During later stages of the relationship, the focus of conflicts shifts to dealing with the responsibilities of parenthood and balancing the needs of the family with the demands of other outside involvements such as career, relatives, and recreation. At this stage, conflicts over sex are reported by couples to be relatively infrequent.

Straus et al. (1981) found that the couples in their survey reported that most conflicts they experienced were about housekeeping. One out of three of the couples stated that they always disagreed over issues such as cooking, cleaning, and other household duties. The other commonly mentioned issues listed in decending order of frequency were: sex, social activities and entertaining, money, and "things about the children." There was also a strong relationship between the amount of conflict reported and incidents of violence. Those couples who experienced the most disagreements had a rate of violence 16 times higher than those with low rates of conflict.

Exercises 27, Conflict Issues Survey, and 28, Treating Family Like Strangers, help to normalize the issues of conflict for clients and lead to a discussion of conflict containment.

APPROACHES TO CONFLICT

Perhaps more important than the issues or the content of the conflict is the approach to conflict resolution the couple adopts. There are different orientations and different tactical approaches that can be applied to conflict. Some approaches will escalate conflict, while others will tend to contain it. Awareness of orientations, tactics, and the process of escalation will help clients identify their own approaches to conflict and to consider alternatives.

Conflict Orientation

Conflict orientation has been analyzed by Mouton and Blake (1971) in terms of the investment in the relationship and investment in personal goals. They describe four major problem-solving orientations that depend on how much a person is motivated by either personal gain or the desire to maintain the relationship. People who are highly motivated to maintain the relationship and to achieve personal gain are called "problem solvers." They assume a problem-solving mode and see conflict as an opportunity to seek acceptable solutions. This approach is trusting, optimistic, and issue oriented. Those who put a high value on personal gain but a low value on the relationship are called "tough battlers." They consider the threat of loss or compromise to be a loss of face. Conflict is conducted in a belligerent, independent, personalized style with no quarter asked for or given. The tough battler is willing to risk the relationship in order to have his position prevail. The "take my marbles" orientation to conflict involves little commitment to either the issue of personal gain or to the relationship. Low risk, low trust, and the tendency to leave rather than struggle for conflict resolution are found in this approach. Finally, those high in commitment to the relationship and low in commitment to personal gain are described as "friendly helpers." Their major concern is to preserve the relationship, and they are willing to give up personal gain to do this. They tend to be trusting, unrealistically optimistic, and dependent.

The most common conflict orientation in abusive relationships occurs when a tough battler is paired with a friendly helper. Often these rigid complementary roles are established early in the relationship and are adhered to out of a fear of abandonment or fear of open conflict, emotional immaturity, or intense dependency. The couple may appear to be stuck in opposite roles such as strong/weak, competent/incompetent, logical/illogical, independent/dependent. As long as these roles are accepted by both parties, violent conflict can be avoided. Violence tends to occur when the complementary nature of the relationship is threatened—usually when the friendly helper has had enough of the subordinate role and attempts to disrupt the system by asserting her independence.

Weitzman and Dreen (1982) have pointed out that the major issues over which battles for control in complementary relationships are likely to occur are distance and intimacy, jealousy and loyalty, dependence and independence, rejection and unconditional acceptance, adequacy and inadequacy, and control, power, and powerlessness. Although these issues are shared by nonviolent couples, it is the rigid relationship roles held by abusive couples and the profound threat to the relationship that is experienced by them when the rules are challenged that makes the eruption of violence so likely.

Conflict Tactics

Another way of viewing conflict is to consider the conflict tactics employed by the couple. In the "win-lose" approach, the person rejects compromise in an effort to win. "I win, you lose" is the motto and since much is seen as riding on the outcome, extreme tactics may be justified. The problem with the win-lose approach is that it is entirely possible to win the round but lose the fight. In a symmetrical relationship where each side perceives itself to be more or less equal, the loser almost always tries to settle the score and return to a position of power, thus perpetuating the conflict. Therefore, the last thing a spouse wants to do in an ongoing relationship is to win an argument.

When this happens, he has only won that particular round, in which case he has about 60 seconds to go to his corner, rest, and get ready for the next round.

The "lose-lose" tactic suggests that "If I can't win, neither will you." Here, when victory is no longer seen as possible, effort is directed at preventing the other from gaining advantage. A variety of passive/aggressive behaviors may be used to this end.

The "win-win" approach is the most desirable tactic for couples to use. Here the goal becomes that of seeking the greatest mutual gain. Negotiation and compromise are used to insure that neither side feels defeated and, thus, feels the need to perpetuate conflict to settle scores. Rather than "my way" versus "your way," the focus is on defeating the issue rather than each other (Mouton & Blake, 1971).

Conflict Escalation

It is helpful for couples to be aware of conflict escalation, or the sequence of stages that occurs as conflict begins to get out of hand. Again, the intent is to provide participants with the nomenclature for understanding conflict.

The conflict escalation model (Stuart, 1980b) indicates that there are three separate stages of conflict that occur sequentially. The first is the *issue* level, where conflict almost always starts. Conflict remains resolvable as long as it can be contained at this level; there is no issue that cannot be discussed and potentially resolved as long as it is discussed with enough care. When couples remain issue focused, they tend to adopt the win-win tactic, focus on the present, define the issue in process terms, confine themselves to "how" questions, define the issue in specific terms using only enough detail and example to clarify rather than overwhelm, focus on just one issue at a time, and maintain a realistic problem-solving perspective.

When arguments escalate they go from an issue level to a *personality* level. It is important to be able to identify when this shift occurs because at that point the focus on the issue itself is lost and resolution of the conflict becomes almost impossible. At the personality level, the win-win tactics are given up for a win-lose approach. Couples return to the past through numerous examples of misconduct or bad faith, blaming is brought into play, opponents become defensive by asking "why" questions, and overgeneralizations ("You always . . . ," "You never . . .") tend to sidetrack the parties. Two other tactics often used at this level are issue expansion, where a whole collection of wrongful behavior and observations on the other's limitations is presented, and crucializing, where the issue becomes just a trivial example of a much more important and insoluable point ("If you really loved me, you would . . ."). Again, at this level the focus is shifted from the original issue to the personalities of the two parties and resolution of the issue becomes almost impossible.

The final level in the conflict escalation model is that of the *relationship*. If the couple has been successful in convincing themselves of all the charges made during the personality level stage, the obvious question becomes "If we are both so hopeless, why do we stay together?" Now the value of attempting to maintain the relationship is questioned, and once that occurs, all restraint is abandoned.

In the following example of conflict escalation, Bill forgot his wife's request that he buy some milk on his way home so that she could fix breakfast the next morning.

ISSUE LEVEL
Jane: *How* are we going to feed the kids tomorrow morning?
Bill: I could borrow some milk from the neighbor or we could fix eggs or we could go out to eat.

PERSONALITY LEVEL
Jane: *Why* did you forget the milk? (Shifts focus to personality and blame) You never do what I ask. You must not think that the family is as important as your work. Your father was the same way.
Bill: (Defensively) I would be able to remember better if I didn't have to work so hard to pay the bills that you create. You are not all that reliable yourself.

RELATIONSHIP LEVEL
Jane: Well, if I'm that unreliable and you are so much more interested in your work than your family, why don't we just get divorced?

It is important for couples to understand the conflict escalation sequence so that they can monitor their own conflicts. An awareness that once the issue focus is lost they will become sidetracked on each other's personalities can serve to keep conflicts issue oriented. Couples should discuss how to prompt each other when the issues focus is being lost and how they should proceed once this occurs.

Exercise 29, Conflict Escalation, has couples analyze one of their recent arguments using the escalation model. The Conflict Escalation Handout can serve as a prompt for the couples.

CONFLICT CONTAINMENT

Once couples have recognized that conflict is inevitable and not necessarily to be feared or avoided, and they have developed an awareness of conflict orientation, conflict tactics, and the process of escalation, they are ready to develop their own approach to conflict containment. The following principles should guide their efforts in this area.

1. Problem solving is a collaborative effort to resolve a mutual problem. Each issue, regardless of who raises it, has implications for the level of satisfaction experienced by both partners. Positive change will benefit both spouses and, thus, all problems are mutually owned (Jacobson & Margolin, 1979).

2. Two winner (win-win) tactics should be used. The problem should be defined in relationship terms and the goal should be to seek a resolution that is acceptable to both partners. An emphasis on "our" issue or saying "we have a problem" will encourage collaboration and reduce defensiveness (Mouton & Blake, 1971).

3. Each partner should follow the change first principle. Rather than insisting that the other party must change first, couples should define the issue in terms of a process with each assuming part of the responsibility for contributing to the conflict (Stuart, 1980b). It is reasonable to assume that if "we" have a problem, there must be something that "I" am doing that serves to maintain it (Harrell & Guerney, 1976). Each party should be prepared to "pay in advance" for positive outcomes by changing his own behavior. To insist that the other change first is to perpetuate a stalemate.

4. Problem solving should consist of two distinct, nonoverlapping phases: problem definition and problem solution. Problem definition should continue until both husband and wife have achieved a clear understanding of the definition of the issues. Negotiation or proposals for change should not be presented until this phase is complete. Once problem definition is accomplished and the couple has moved on to problem solution, they should not redefine the issues or introduce additional issues. In this way the tendency to counter one complaint with another is avoided (Jacobson & Margolin, 1979).

5. Problem definition should be brief, positive, specific, and present oriented. Couples often confuse talking about a problem with problem resolution. Talking about the problem may involve listing numerous examples of the problem behavior (which invites debate over the details as they are recalled and presented) or attempting to come up with the cause. The issue should be presented in terms of specific observations about the other's behavior (process language), not personality (terminal language) with specific recommendations for change. Couples who experience difficulty in giving up derogatory, terminal language ("Stop being so lazy, stupid, frigid") are probably more concerned with vengeance than problem solving.

6. Only one problem at a time should be discussed. Issues should be broken down into small, solvable steps and couples should avoid getting sidetracked on other issues. Couples often try to tackle big problems before they have practiced their skills on smaller issues or attempt to move from one problem to the next. They should instead attempt to deal with only one issue at each sitting.

7. The communication skills of listening, validation, feeling-talk, positive expression, and negative feeling expression should be used. By paraphrasing or summarizing the other's statements, couples should focus attention, avoid interruptions, demonstrate respect, and make any misunderstandings immediately apparent.

8. Problem solving should be modest, mutual, and future oriented. When they finish defining the problem and begin to work on solutions, clients should recognize that they won't get everything they want. The best solutions will be expressed in the spirit of mutual cooperation, with each party investing something in the change process. Clients should practice brainstorming a number of possible alternatives before attempting to reach closure, and avoid returning to the past and to those activities involved in the definition phase.

9. Conclusions should be detailed and repeated by each partner to insure that agreement has actually been reached.

Clients may want to make notes on the Conflict Containment Principles Handout while each point is discussed and demonstrated. When they use these principles in a conflict situation, couples should try not to extend the process beyond about 45 minutes. After reaching the conclusion to an issue, they should congratulate themselves and take a break before discussing another problem.

Frequently, couples report that the process of conflict escalation occurs largely outside their awareness and that by the time they realize they have reached the danger point, it is very hard to de-escalate the level of conflict. It may be helpful to review the provisions of the Time-out Contract developed in Session 1 to reassure both parties that the process of conflict escalation can be terminated as they begin to practice conflict-containment skills. Much of the discussion material on conflict orientation, tactics, and escalation is intended to provide clients with the labels and framework required to define and discriminate this process of conflict escalation. Exercise 30, Dirty Fighting

Techniques, is a particularly effective method for labeling certain behavior patterns. Couples quickly recognize tactics that lead to escalation when they are presented in an exaggerated manner. The Dirty Fighting Techniques Handout helps couples when role playing these tactics. The Dirty Fighting Score Sheet can be used for prompting and scoring. When couples acquire a nomenclature for analyzing conflict, they can prompt each other when the tactics are first introduced in a conflict and avoid escalation. Exercise 31, Applying Skills, which uses the Communication Prompting and Evaluating Worksheet (Chapter Seven) and the Conflict Containment Principles Handout, can be assigned to clients as homework to practice communication and conflict-containment skills.

EXERCISE 27

CONFLICT ISSUES SURVEY

After reviewing the sources of intrafamily conflict to normalize the issue of conflict in marriage, ask couples which issues they fight over the most. Tabulate the results when working with a group. This exercise can be a good introduction to the topic of conflict containment because it establishes the fact that the focus should not be on whether there is conflict, but rather on how to resolve and contain the inevitable conflicts as they occur.

EXERCISE 28

TREATING FAMILY LIKE STRANGERS

The observation has been made that we often treat strangers with more civility and respect than we treat members of our own families. Ask clients to consider why this might be the case and list all the reasons offered. Examples may include:

1. It is easy to put up with strangers knowing that you may not have to see them again, but you think that you will have to put up with a spouse forever.
2. We think that certain chores are the spouse's duty and therefore don't merit thanks.
3. The issues that spouses have to agree on are much more important than issues in other relationships.
4. You can't get away from your spouse and cool off as easily as you can get away from other people; you can't leave and go home if you are already there.

EXERCISE 29

CONFLICT ESCALATION

Ask couples to apply the conflict-escalation model to an analysis of one of their recent arguments. Have them identify the statements that signaled the shift from the issue to the personality level. They can use

EXERCISE 29 (cont.)

the Conflict Escalation Handout as a prompt. Develop the following points from their examples:

1. Conflict almost always starts at the issue level.
2. If the conflict is contained at the issue level, resolution is possible.
3. Once the couple leaves the issue level for the personality level, it is unlikely that the issue will ever be resolved.

EXERCISE 30

DIRTY FIGHTING TECHNIQUES

Distribute and review the Dirty Fighting Techniques Handout. Invite clients to discuss and give examples of their favorite techniques. Have the clients role play a conflict situation using as many dirty fighting techniques as possible.

In a group setting, a dirty fighting tournament can be held by giving each couple a conflict situation to role play and having the rest of the group score the couple on how many dirty techniques they are able to use in a fixed period of time. It may be advisable to have clients pair up with someone other than their spouses because they may become too involved in the content of the argument, particularly if it is similar to an issue that they have actually fought about. The Dirty Fighting Score Sheet can be used as a prompt and as a means of keeping score by the group.

Each situation should also be role played using conflict-containment principles. (This portion of the exercise is usually not entered into with the same degree of enthusiasm as the dirty fighting portion.)

EXERCISE 31

APPLYING SKILLS

Ask couples to choose two areas of conflict and attempt to apply their communication and problem-solving skills to these areas during the week. Ask each to keep notes on the exercise and grade himself (not spouse) on the use of the skills contained on the Communication Prompting and Evaluating Worksheet (Chapter Seven) and the Conflict Containment Principles Handout.

CONFLICT ESCALATION HANDOUT

ISUE ⟶	PERSONALITY ⟶	RELATIONSHIP
Win-win	Win-lose	Lose-lose
Present	Past	If we are both
Mutual ownership	Blame	so lousy, why stay
"How" questions	"Why" questions	together
Specific	Overgeneralized ("You always . . ., never . . .")	
Focused	Issue expansion	
Realistic perspective	Crucializing ("If you love me . . .")	

CONFLICT CONTAINMENT PRINCIPLES HANDOUT

1. Problem solving is a collaborative effort to resolve a mutual problem.

2. Two winner (win-win) tactics should be used.

3. Each partner should follow the change first principle.

4. Problem solving should consist of two distinct, nonoverlapping phases: problem definition and problem solution.

5. Problem definition should be brief, positive, specific, and present oriented.

6. Only one problem at a time should be discussed.

7. The communication skills of listening, validation, feeling-talk, positive expression, and negative feeling expression should be used.

8. Problem solving should be modest, mutual, and future oriented.

9. Conclusions should be detailed and repeated by each partner.

DIRTY FIGHTING TECHNIQUES HANDOUT

1. *Timing*—Pick the right time to begin an argument. Late at night, during a favorite TV show, after several drinks, or just before your spouse has to leave for work are options. As a general rule, look for the time your spouse least expects it or is least able to respond.

2. *Escalating*—Move quickly from the issue, to questioning of personality, to wondering whether it is worth the effort to stay together (issue to personality to relationship). Interpret your spouse's shortcomings as evidence of bad faith and the impossibility of a happy relationship.

3. *Brown Bagging*—Try to list as many problems in as much detail as possible. Don't stick to the original issue, but rather throw in all the problems you can think of. Don't limit yourself to the present. If your partner can't recall the offense, so much the better.

4. *Overgeneralizing*—Use words like "always" and "never" as in "You are always late." This is likely to distract your partner into discussing the overgeneralization rather than the issue and insure further misunderstandings.

5. *Cross-complaining*—Respond to any complaint your spouse may raise with one of your own. For example, "Me late? Why, if it weren't for the fact that you never have any clean clothes for me. . . ." If done properly you can balance complaint against complaint forever.

6. *Crucializing*—Exaggerate the importance of the issue with statements such as "If you really loved us, you would never have done it in the first place" or "This proves that you don't care." Never concede that an issue is not absolutely critical and in need of immediate resolution.

7. *Asking Why*—"Why didn't you clean up?" or "Why were you late?" will imply that there must be something terribly wrong with your spouse and that something more than simple problem behavior that might be easily resolved is at issue.

8. *Blaming*—Make it clear that the fault lies entirely with your spouse and that once again you are simply the innocent victim. Don't admit that your behavior plays any part in the difficulty. Make sure your spouse realizes that you will not change first.

DIRTY FIGHTING TECHNIQUES HANDOUT (cont.)

9. *Pulling Rank*—Rather than depend on the merits of your argument, pull rank by reminding your partner that you make more money, have more education, are older or younger, or are wiser or more experienced in such matters. Anything that will enhance your status at your spouse's expense should be considered.

10. *Not Listening, Dominating*—Any time you appear to be listening you run the risk of suggesting that you value your partner's opinion. Consider talking while your spouse is talking, pretending to read, or falling asleep.

11. *Listing Injustices*—This is a great morale builder. By reciting every slight injustice or inequity you have suffered in the relationship, you will experience a renewed sense of self-righteousness. You can use this approach to justify almost any activity you have always wanted to engage in. For example, "Since you went ahead and bought that dress, I can buy a new car."

12. *Labeling*—By labeling somebody in a negative manner, you can create the impression that that person is totally at fault. Psychological labels, such as "childish," "neurotic," "insecure," or "alcoholic," are particularly effective in obscuring issues where you may be vulnerable.

13. *Mind-reading*—By deciding that you know the *real* reason why someone is acting in a certain way, you can avoid having to debate issues. For example, "You only said that to set me up" or "You don't really feel that way" are particularly effective.

14. *Fortune-telling*—Predicting the future can save you the effort of really trying to resolve problems. "You will never change" or "It would be easy for me to change, but you wouldn't live up to it" are statements that can protect you from having to make any effort at all.

15. *Being Sarcastic*—This is a great way of saying something without having to take responsibility for it. If you can say, "You're so smart . . ." just right, you can imply that your spouse is stupid and deny that you said it at the same time.

DIRTY FIGHTING TECHNIQUES HANDOUT (cont.)

16. *Avoiding Responsibility*—Although not a very elegant tactic, saying "I don't remember" can bring the discussion to an abrupt halt. Alcohol or fatigue can serve the same purpose as in "I must have been drunk."

17. *Leaving*—No problem is so big or important that it can't be ignored. Walk out of the room, leave home, or just refuse to talk. Sometimes just threatening to leave can accomplish the same ends without the inconvenience involved in actually leaving.

18. *Rejecting Compromise*—Don't back down. Why settle for compromise when with a little luck you can really devastate your spouse (and destroy the relationship). Stick with the "one winner" philosophy.

19. *Personalizing*—Anybody can resolve a conflict by sticking to the issue. Shift to personalities and you should be able to generate enough defensiveness to keep the conflict going forever.

20. *Playing the Martyr*—If timed properly, this tactic can completely disorient the opposition. "You're right dear, I am hopeless" can stop your spouse cold. An example of a less subtle form is "How could you say that after all I've done for you?" An extreme form is to threaten to kill yourself if your spouse doesn't shape up.

21. *Using Money*—"If you made as much money as . . ." or "When you make as much as I do, then you can have an opinion" are old favorites.

22. *Using Children*—"If you spent more time with them, they wouldn't be failing" or "Do you want them to grow up like you?" can always be used unless you are so unfortunate as to have perfect children.

23. *Using Relatives*—"When you do that, you are just like your mother" can be used to break your spouse's concentration and undermine confidence.

24. *Giving Advice*—By telling people how to act, think, and feel, you can maintain a position of superiority while insisting that you are only trying to be helpful.

DIRTY FIGHTING TECHNIQUES HANDOUT (cont.)

25. *Getting Even*—Don't settle for a compromise or an apology. Hold grudges for as long as possible; you might need those complaints in future arguments.

26. *Using Terminal Language*—For example, if you happen to be upset by the fact that the room wasn't straightened, start with "You slob . . ." to suggest that it is your spouse's existence and not behavior that is at question.

27. *Being Inconsistent*—Keep your spouse off balance by changing your position. Try complaining that your spouse never talks to you and then ignore whatever your spouse says.

28. *Others*—This list should only be considered suggestive of the range of tactics to be drawn from. With practice and creativity, you should be able to come up with numerous innovations.

DIRTY FIGHTING SCORE SHEET

Score one point for each technique that is used.

Couple # _____

TACTIC	SCORE	COMMENT
1. Timing		
2. Escalating		
3. Brown bagging		
4. Overgeneralizing		
5. Cross-complaining		
6. Crucializing		
7. Asking why		
8. Blaming		
9. Pulling rank		
10. Not listening, dominating		
11. Listing injustices		
12. Labeling		
13. Mind-reading		
14. Fortune-telling		
15. Being sarcastic		
16. Avoiding responsibility		
17. Leaving		
18. Rejecting compromise		
19. Personalizing		
20. Playing the martyr		

DIRTY FIGHTING SCORE SHEET (cont.)

TACTIC	SCORE	COMMENT
21. Using money		
22. Using children		
23. Using relatives		
24. Giving advice		
25. Getting even		
26. Using terminal language		
27. Being inconsistent		
28. Others		

Chapter Nine

Jealousy, Sex Role Stereotyping, and Marital Dependency

The interrelated issues of jealousy, rigid sex role stereotyping, and marital dependency are often particularly troublesome for abusive couples. Sexual doubts and insecurities can contribute significantly to marital conflict, and expressions of jealousy are among the most common precipitants of violent episodes. These topics, because they are so conflict laden, are addressed late in the course of treatment. It is important that couples have had an opportunity to practice communication and conflict-containment skills before dealing with the material in this chapter.

JEALOUSY

Although jealousy can be found to some degree in all relationships, it frequently plays a particularly important role in abusive situations. Jealousy is defined as that state of mind arising from the suspicion, apprehension, or knowledge of the unfaithfulness of a wife, husband, or lover, or the fear of being replaced or diminished in importance in the affections of a significant other. It can be experienced more or less exclusively as a sexual threat, or more broadly as a fear of displacement. Factors that seem to affect the susceptibility to jealousy include the length and stability of the relationship; the maturity, dependence, and level of self-esteem of the individuals; their expectations for emotional gratification; and the perceived availability of alternatives to the primary relationship. Constantine (1976) has suggested that an individual's sense of security within a relationship operates as a "threshold mechanism," determining the extent to which any particular situation will be perceived as threatening. A number of the factors that place people at risk to experience jealousy are characteristic of those couples involved in spouse abuse. Additionally, skill deficits in the areas of communication and conflict containment make it likely that the experience of jealousy will lead to potentially violent conflict.

This is compounded by the fact that abusive people are often members of a subculture that condones anger and violence as an appropriate response to jealousy. As Whitehurst (1971) has observed, there is still no socially accepted alternative to anger or violence in situations of real or even suspected infidelity.

It is helpful to normalize the potentially emotion-laden topic of jealousy by presenting it as an issue that all marriages are confronted with, and one that all couples need to be aware of and give some thought to; as such, it is not an affliction people either have or don't have, but simply one more issue to be dealt with in any marriage. The film *Shifting Gears* available from O.D.N. Productions, 74 Varick St., Room 304, New York, NY 10013, is an excellent vehicle for triggering the discussion of jealousy.

Examples of jealousy unrelated to sexuality are often considerably easier to work with initially. A common example that can be used is the feeling of exclusion, threat, or jealousy a spouse may experience, particularly early in marriage, because of his partner's continuing attachment to her family of origin. This can be a problem especially during holiday visits to relatives' homes. The therapist can also normalize jealousy by discussing such situations from his own experience. In addition to desexualizing jealousy, substituting neutral or even positive terms for the more negative language often employed by couples can serve to cast the issue in a new light. Teismann (1979) suggests using words such as *romantic, passionate, loyal, devoted,* and *sensitive* rather than *possessive, dependent, paranoid, insecure,* and *irrational* to alter the perspective clients may assume toward this subject. He also suggests emphasizing the interactional nature of jealousy as opposed to an individual pathology model.

It is also helpful to indicate that jealousy can serve several positive functions: it tends to define the limits of the relationship at a level of complexity that the couple can be comfortable with, it communicates caring and commitment to the relationship, and it can serve as an early warning signal of insecurity or negative feelings about the condition of the relationship. Jealousy becomes problematic when it is expressed indirectly, is experienced compulsively, becomes irrational, or leads to extreme levels of vigilance and control.

Some of the most serious manifestations of jealousy occur in cases of pathological bonding. Here one or both spouses cling desperately to the other, viewing the outside world with apprehension and suspicion. It is as if their own boundaries and sense of self are so weak that separation from the spouse is experienced as a threat to their own existence. In these cases, they respond as if separation is life threatening, and will go to almost any length to maintain the relationship.

Although such cases are relatively rare, they are encountered and constitute some risk of homicide or suicide when separation occurs.

A much less serious threat is posed by those complementary relationships in which spouses are attracted to each other because they sense that each possesses characteristics that the other is lacking. These relationships are inherently unstable as the differences tend to become exaggerated over time. For example, it is not uncommon for a dominating, insecure male to form a relationship with a passive, dependent female. Problems begin to occur when these qualities of passivity, which are often also accompanied by a general ineptness, begin to annoy rather than attract the male. Although passive females are not threatening, they also frequently are not particularly effective at parenting or other responsibilities. Difficulties escalate when each individual engages in more of the same behavior to correct the problem. The passive wife, sensing that it was her passivity that originally attracted her husband, may become more passive, and the husband may become more controlling and dominating.

In this situation, where efforts at growth, independence, and self-enhancing activity are not met with encouragement, expressions of affection and support from outside parties can be particularly attractive. The husband's awareness of this fact often leads him to be even more controlling and suspicious, and the stage is set for jealousy to escalate.

Men and women seem to experience jealousy somewhat differently, and these differences can lead to feelings of confusion and to being misunderstood (Farber, 1976). Both men and women are likely to feel threatened by the possibility of being displaced. Women are more likely to be concerned about the stability of the relationship. For women, sexual betrayal is symbolic of the threat of being replaced in the relationship. They may also become jealous of their husband's family, friends, TV, or involvement in work. Because this concern is generally outside of the experience of the male, he may react in a surprised or insensitive manner. For men, it is the sexual act itself that threatens their sense of pride and self-worth. Men are more likely to make specific sexual accusations when they feel any sort of threat to the relationship.

When either party feels threatened, two sets of emotions are elicited. The primary emotions elicited are generally fear and insecurity. These primary emotions are followed quickly by anger and usually only this secondary emotion is overtly expressed. Males tend to express their anger directly. The violent expression of jealousy by males is still somewhat socially acceptable. Women are more likely to express their anger indirectly through the withdrawal of affection or other passive/aggressive gestures. The cultural factor of wives' economic dependence and women's relative lack of physical strength may inhibit more direct expressions of anger.

Jealousy seems to be problematic for abusive males and for military men in particular. Military men work in a male-dominated society where masculine values and posturing prevail. Typically, they ascribe to very rigid and traditional views of marriage and sex role stereotypes. They view marriage as a lifelong, exclusive commitment for their wives and, therefore, any hint of infidelity represents a rejection of the marriage itself. Work relationships involve considerable covert, if not overt, sexualizing in the form of joking, story telling, bragging, and flirting. The sense of "bad faith" or defensiveness over their own conduct is often projected onto the wives in the form of suspicion and accusations.

Issues in the Treatment of Jealousy

These considerations about jealousy have implications for the content of treatment in the following ways.

1. Jealousy needs to be normalized and defused in treatment. It is obvious that the issue of jealousy has relevance for a program intended to reduce domestic violence. The topic needs to be addressed, but because it is a potentially explosive issue, it should be dealt with in a measured fashion. It is likely that most abusive couples will have had conflicts over the issues of jealousy, trust, sexual conduct, and control, and that they have expressed these concerns primarily on the topic of sexuality. For this reason, jealousy is first discussed as a normal part of all relationships in a context well removed from the difficult area of sex.

Distancing can be accomplished by discussing jealousy as it applies to the process of breaking away from the family of origin and establishing a new family. When each man marries his wife, he marries a woman who is a member of another family. The history of experiences and relationships in her family of origin have to be in some way left behind and a new family established. However, the old ties and allegiances persist and a balance between the investment in the new family and the continuing relationship with the old must be dealt with. In this situation, it is normal for a husband to experience some sense of competition, unease, and even jealousy over his wife's continuing relationship with her family. The topics of how much contact is acceptable, how rigid the boundaries surrounding the new marriage should be, and how her involvement with her family compares to his involvement with his family permit the discussion of jealousy in a normal, nonsexualized context.

The sexual element can be gradually introduced by describing how marriage is a dynamic, constantly changing relationship. It is important for couples to realize that they can't expect to get everything they want in marriage or in any relationship and to expect that any single relationship can fulfill all of anyone's needs for affiliation, companionship, and stimulation is to impose upon it a burden it cannot survive. Novelty will continue to have an attraction; it is perfectly normal to be attracted to and fantasize about others. The distinction between thought and behavior is important to maintain, with thoughts of sexual attraction being both normal and acceptable and, in themselves, posing no threat to the primary relationship.

2. Clients need to realize that the marriage relationship is constantly changing with a normal pattern that fluctuates between being close and caring and then tending to drift somewhat apart. Couples should recognize that when they are feeling somewhat out-of-tune or apart, their behavior toward each other may change. They are likely to engage in fewer small behaviors that signal commitment and caring, and the feeling of apartness increases.

During these periods of feeling apart, couples are particularly susceptible to jealousy. When their level of current satisfaction with the primary relationship is considerably below that of an alternative relationship or something experienced in the past, they are vulnerable to outside attractions and the stage is set for jealousy.

The experience of jealousy, then, can serve the positive function of signaling that some sort of corrective action is required. When a partner is jealous, positive behavior change (i.e., increasing caring behaviors, spending time with his spouse, engaging in courting behaviors) is a better response to his jealousy than negative prohibitions (i.e., threats, accusations, displays of anger). Expressing his jealousy through anger and attempts to control leads at best to reluctant compliance and at worst to acts of defiance.

3. Jealousy is a secondary emotion. The sequence of the expression of jealousy can be represented like this:

		Experience:		Expression:
	Interpreted	fear,		anger,
Event $\longrightarrow$	as $\longrightarrow$	insecurity,	$\longrightarrow$	threats,
	threat	pain		control

An event may be interpreted as a threat because of relationship rules or cultural mores. Almost invariably, the emotion experienced initially following a threat (spouse appears attracted outside of the primary relationship) is that of anxiety and insecurity. The extent of this insecurity is based on the factors mentioned earlier such as length and stability of the relationship and the maturity and self-esteem of the individuals. This emotion is quickly covered over and what is overtly expressed is anger through withdrawal or increased efforts at controlling the partner. The typical response, in turn, to expressions of anger, is defensiveness. What was expressed in an effort to preserve the relationship may have the opposite effect. If the primary emotion of insecurity could be expressed, however, the spouse might then react with reassurance and the couple could use problem solving to enhance their relationship.

A role play of a jealous situation first expressing the primary emotion and then the secondary emotion can make this point. For example, the primary emotion could be expressed this way:

"You know, when you were talking to _____ last night, I felt sort of anxious. It really is important to me that we get along, and sometimes I get worried."

The secondary emotion could be expressed this way:

"I saw you talking to _____ and it really makes me furious. I've told you I don't appreciate that sort of thing. If I catch you at it again, I'm going to . . ."

The recipients of these two messages would probably feel and respond quite differently.

The lesson is clear: anxiety precedes anger in the jealousy sequence, but is quickly suppressed, and the expression of anger contributes to the problematic situation. Sharing our anxiety may be difficult, but it is likely to be more productive than anger.

Exercise 32, Putting Primary Emotions into Words, helps clients identify and express primary emotions instead of anger when jealous.

4. Males and females are predisposed to experience jealousy differently. As a general rule, men tend to experience and to express jealousy in sexual terms. Even if what they originally experience is a sense that the marriage is drifting apart, the expression of that concern may take the form of an accusation of sexual infidelity. Women, on the other hand, are likely to be concerned about the preservation of the relationship in broader terms and to express this more indirectly. For example, a jealous husband might ask, "Are you having an affair?" while a jealous wife might ask, "Don't you like the way I look anymore?" If both could interpret the other's jealous behavior in positive terms as an expression of commitment to the relationship (relabeling), the destructive potential of jealousy could be minimized.

Exercise 33, Jealousy Role Reversal, demonstrates through role plays that each spouse is likely to react somewhat differently to the same jealousy-provoking situation.

5. Jealousy is expressed through efforts to control as well as through accusations. It is important to discuss the paradoxical nature of control: the more control you try to exercise in a relationship, the less you actually have. A common example of how an attempt at control actually contributes to jealousy and insecurity is when a husband suspects his wife of infidelity because she no longer confides in him and begins to interrogate her concerning how she spends her time. She responds to this intrusion by deliberately withholding information, which heightens his insecurity. The paradoxical nature of control can be demonstrated through role playing a situation in which compliance is demanded and then cooperation is requested.

Another area for discussion is the issue of power. Relationships are usually most satisfying when there is a more-or-less equitable and reciprocal distribution of power—where neither party's will automatically prevails in all situations. The least-loss principle, the idea that the person in a relationship who has less invested or has the least to lose has the most power, suggests that jealousy and involvement outside the primary relationship can significantly alter the balance of power in a relationship.

It may be useful to discuss the fact that in addition to being counterproductive, extreme efforts at control are generally undesirable. Invariably, relationships such as master/slave, jailer/prisoner, and owner/pet come to mind. Most men do not really want to control either their wives or their children, although they may occasionally lose sight of this fact. Exercise 34, Exercising Control, uses exaggeration to show the ineffectiveness of efforts of control.

Intervention Strategies

The issue of trust is often raised when some sort of betrayal or sexual infidelity has occurred. For couples who find themselves in this situation, the choice is fairly straightforward: they can choose to give in to vengeance or they can choose to move ahead with relationship enhancement, but they can't do both. As a general rule, couples should understand that for a relationship to have any chance of improving, three conditions must exist (Stuart, 1980a):

1. They must be able to live in the present, putting the past in the past.

2. They must contain their anger and give up efforts at punishment.
3. They must suspend doubt and proceed on the possibility (not the certainty) that things can improve.

If these preconditions for positive change cannot be met, there is not much chance for improvement.

It is helpful to label trust in process terms and to indicate that in certain conditions it is natural that mistrust will temporarily prevail. Trustworthiness is *not* a trait that some people possess and some don't, but it is a function of a person's history of behavior. Defining trust as the ability to confidently make positive predictions about another's behavior reinforces thinking of it as a process. To have difficulty trusting someone is perfectly natural under certain conditions. Lack of trust should be accepted as natural and temporary and the couple should be encouraged to get on with the business of relationship enhancement if that is their choice.

"Pathological jealousy," where one spouse experiences unfounded, intense jealousy that reaches almost delusional proportions, is both rare and potentially serious. This situation should be carefully assessed and a referral for additional treatment considered. It is fairly easy to detect people who are fixated on the topic of infidelity, as they cannot be diverted or distracted from discussions of it. Efforts at surveillance and other jealous rituals can be seen as superstitious behavior. Over time, the jealous individual who engages in a number of these acts may come to believe that it is the rituals themselves that are preventing the partner's infidelity (Jacobson & Margolin, 1979). Obviously, to abandon the ritual would be seen as a significant risk. The jealous partner should be encouraged to experiment with reducing the rituals and should be rewarded at each step by the failure of infidelity to occur. The spouse should play an active part in this approach by reinforcing with positive behavior any reduction in efforts to control and in overt expression of jealousy.

Frequently, irrational beliefs and automatic thoughts can be identified that fuel any type of jealousy and these can be approached using the cognitive methods previously introduced for anger control. The belief that spouses should be able to meet all of each other's needs for friendship and intellectual stimulation and that the relationship is failing if either spouse desires any additional friendship is one example of a belief that can lead to jealousy. Clients can refute this belief by realizing that no one person can meet all of any other person's needs. Clients may also think that if their spouses show any interest in others it means that their spouses will no longer love them and that they are bound to leave. This can be refuted by pointing out that it is natural for spouses to be interested in and attracted to other people sometimes, but that it doesn't mean they will want to leave the relationship.

Another irrational belief that may make people jealous is the belief that if they lose a relationship, they would be doomed to be lonely forever because no one else could possibly love them. Clients can deal with this by realizing that they cannot predict the future, that there is always the possibility of being loved again, and that being alone does not mean they would be miserable.

A husband may also believe that his wife's unfaithfulness would reflect badly on him (people would assume he is a terrible lover, etc.). The husband with this belief dwells on how bad he would look if this were to occur and how worthless he would feel, rather than on the unfaithfulness itself. Statements such as the following can help counter this irrational belief: "I'm still just as worthwhile no matter what my wife does or what other people might think" and "This type of thing is unpleasant, but it happens to a lot of people. I can cope with it."

Clients can be assigned to use the Anger Log II, to record incidents of jealousy as homework to gain practice in identifying and refuting the irrational thoughts that lead to jealousy.

SEX ROLE STEREOTYPING

A discussion of the influence of sex role stereotyping will assist couples in detecting the influence of stereotypes on their thinking and reduce the influence of extreme and rigid sex roles. As Bem (1977a) has pointed out, being masculine or feminine is a value that can have considerable influence on self-esteem. "In American society, men are supposed to be masculine, women are supposed to be feminine, and neither sex is supposed to be much like the other" (p. 103). Men are traditionally expected to be tough, independent, and self-reliant, all qualities that will enable them to carry out their responsibility to support and to protect their families. Their success can be measured in terms of their ability to defend, financially provide for, and keep the family from having to work too hard, either in the home or the marketplace. To engage in feminine behavior, then, is to risk being considered unsuccessful, unmasculine, or even to have their sexual orientation or preference questioned.

Women are expected to be tender, sympathetic, and sensitive to the needs of others. They are to develop the nurturant skills necessary to meet the emotional needs of the family and to maintain harmonious interactions among family members (Spence & Helmreich, 1978).

Additionally, they are to be prepared (but not too prepared) to assume the duties of the husband in his absence.

Couples with a history of domestic violence may experience conflict because they believe in these rigid, narrowly defined, traditional sex roles.

1. They impose excessively high sex role standards on themselves, which they are unable to attain. They experience insecurity, doubt, and stress when these roles are not achieved or sustained.

2. They define the range of permissible sex-linked behavior rigidly, which does not permit cooperation or adaptability. This makes it difficult to share in household tasks or respond flexibly when circumstance requires some alteration in the division of labor. It also makes it likely that the relationship will be defined in terms of task accomplishment, and the stage is set for conflicts over who is working the hardest.

3. They experience conflicts over emotional expressiveness, affection, and companionship when these behaviors are equated with the feminine role.

4. They cling to traditional values that are being challenged by the larger society and that may place them at odds with family and friends.

5. They tend to respond to each other on the basis of their stereotypes about what members of the opposite sex want and are like rather than checking out what their partners really want and are like.

Women who adopt a role of extreme femininity may sacrifice their own welfare out of an exaggerated concern for others. They are likely to be afraid to be assertive, to exercise leadership, or to trust their own judgment. They may be excessively dependent. Men who assume a position of extreme masculinity may, in their failure to consider the needs of others, tend to exploit and dominate. They are inclined to reject "feminine" behaviors such as crying, touching, and admitting to fear and weakness. As Bem (1977b) points out, it is entirely possible to be both masculine and feminine and even to combine the traditional masculine emphasis on task accomplishment with the traditional feminine emphasis on the concern for others in a single act. For example, it is possible to fire an employee when that is required, but to do it in a way that considers the feelings such an act is likely to produce.

Exercise 35, Sex Role Characteristics, helps clients see a mixture of traditionally masculine and feminine characteristics as desirable.

Sexuality

In addition to general sex role differences, a number of traditional beliefs about sexuality can cause problems for couples. It is not uncommon, particularly for abusive males, to have beliefs and ideals concerning sexual performance that can contribute greatly to their insecurity. Husbands may adopt the belief that males have a constant, high-level sex drive, that they are like machines that are always turned on (Nowinski, 1980). They may believe that it is their responsibility to arouse their partners and that they themselves should require no courting or stimulation and experience no performance difficulties. The myth that male sexuality is "simple, straightforward, and problem-free" can lead men to adopt "superhuman standards by which to measure their equipment, performance, and satisfaction, thus ensuring a perpetual no-win situation" (Zilbergeld, 1978, p. 8). Women seem to be much less likely to equate sexual performance with self-esteem or to feel as personally threatened when sexual difficulties are experienced. However, they may contribute to their husband's insecurity if they believe in and communicate rigid sexual-performance standards for him.

Insecurity can lead males into extreme postures of masculinity and aggressive sexuality that are difficult to sustain and that will create more insecurity and stress on both themselves and their marriages. For example, a male who is preoccupied with reaching a high level of sexual performance would also experience a high level of anxiety that the goal might not be achieved. Because of his anxiety about sexual performance, he is at risk to experience some sort of sexual dysfunction. If he were to fail to maintain an erection, he would probably find this profoundly threatening, and his anxiety would make it more likely that the difficulty would reoccur. Doubts about his masculinity and his ability to "fulfill his wife" would predispose him to the experience of jealousy and the likelihood of violence would be increased.

Exercise 36, Sex Attitudes, uses the Sex Attitude Worksheet to promote discussion of the more common anxiety-inducing sexual myths.

Dominance in Marriage

Marriage is traditionally seen, at least by some abusive husbands, as a hierarchical relationship which should be headed by the husband. One potential source of conflict occurs when men who believe they must maintain their status as head of the household feel they are in a secondary or subservient role. They may then experience significant cognitive dissonance and resentment, and may resort to violence to regain the dominant position. In many cases, this occurs even though men don't particularly want to dominate; they simply feel they should, or that others expect that of them.

Gelles (1972) and Rounsaville (1978) have found that "status inconsistency" was present more frequently in violent than in nonviolent families. Status inconsistency was operationally defined as occurring whenever the husband was less educated, less verbal, made less money than his wife, or had failed to achieve a desired occupational level. This finding is consistent with the resource theory of violence that states that violence is a resource, or tool, that will be used to maintain a position of authority when other resources turn out to be insufficient. Dominance is usually maintained in any relationship through social sanction and the competency of those of higher status. This is particularly true in the family, where, as Goode (1971) pointed out, the use of force can result in the loss of spontaneous respect and affection. Therefore, the more resources (for example, social prestige, salary, education) the husband possesses in relation to other family members, the less likely it is that overt force will be employed.

Rounsaville (1978) investigated the related concept of "role reversal" by asking battered women to compare their performance with that of their mate on eight tasks: housework, child care, grocery shopping, car repairs, bill paying, social arranging, decision making, and income earning. The women rated themselves as superior to their husbands in all areas except that of car repairs. Although no figures were presented on the number of nonbattered wives who feel the same way, it was suggested that this "role reversal" may contribute to domestic violence.

Goldberg (1976) observed that men often turn over more and more responsibility to their wives, only to then resent the wives' function as the permission giver and eventually lash out in a desperate effort to regain control. Clients frequently report violent episodes precipitated by arguments over finances. Husbands may turn the bookkeeping and financial responsibilities over to their wives and then at some point feel like children and become enraged when they have to ask for money or find that they can't afford a purchase.

Most conflict over dominance is manifested at the practical level over two specific functions or skills: request making and decision making. As discussed in Chapter Seven, requests can be made positively, promoting cooperation and compliance, or as commands that elicit resentment and rebellion. Regardless of who is seen as dominant in a relationship, no one likes to be ordered to do something. Reviewing the principles of positive request making and role playing requests first using demands or commands and then using positive requests reminds clients which methods are most likely to secure the desired level of compliance.

There is often a surprising amount of agreement between spouses about who should make decisions. The three models of decision making are:

1. Authoritarian. One spouse makes decisions or specifically delegates authority to decide.
2. Democratic. Both spouses have input and decisions are based on consensus.
3. Specialized. Authority is divided between spouses according to areas of expertise.

Usually most couples say they prefer the democratic option with few expressing the desire for a husband-dominated, authoritarian model when asked to specify how decisions are to be made. Occasionally, this will be followed by the concern that the democratic model won't always work and that someone must be prepared to assume responsibility when deadlock occurs. However, they are usually unable to give specific examples of when this was required in the past. Often the husband dominates decision making although the spouses say they prefer the democratic model. This may be because they do not have the communication skills to implement the democratic model.

There are many disagreements and misunderstandings that can exist over decision making. It is better to have open disagreement over decision making so the possibility of resolution exists than for misunderstandings to continue. Misunderstandings may include areas of "pseudosuperiority" where one partner believes he has authority, but it is not acknowledged by the spouse, or "pseudoinferiority" where a partner feels without authority when the spouse has, in fact, granted the responsibility (Stuart, 1980b). Occasionally, both parties may indicate that the other is currently making the decisions in a certain area. For example, the husband may indicate that his wife decides when to have sex, and she may state that he does. In these cases, there is probably a subtle exchange of signals and simply clearing up the communication pattern will enable both to experience more power.

Not all conflicts have to do with the desire to assume increased authority. Frequently, neither spouse wants responsibility (for example, to handle the finances), and misunderstandings arise when the decision gets "dropped through the cracks."

Exercise 37, Decision Making, asks clients to choose the model of decision making they prefer in part A and uses the Decision Making Worksheet to enable them to see how they now make decisions in their relationship in part B.

MARITAL DEPENDENCY

The question of why people continue to stay in abusive or unsatisfying marriages is often raised. This is particularly true in cases of instrumental violence, where the occurrence of violence has become rather predictable. As has been noted earlier, the remorse and sorrow, together with shifts in power and the evident desire to eliminate violence from the relationship, that follow the acute violent episode can serve to sustain optimism and perpetuate the relationship. However, in cases of instrumental violence, hope has been eroded and replaced by a pervasive sense of hopelessness and apathy. Perpetrator and victim roles are fixed, and the victim, who in instrumental violence is almost always the wife, is likely to become markedly fearful, withdrawn, and insecure. Although a realistic appraisal of her situation would suggest that permanent separation is the most appropriate course, the couple may cling to each other and actively resist any attempt at intervention. The wife often shows symptoms of "learned helplessness" and the prognosis that she will successfully leave the relationship is quite guarded. In those more common situations where the couple is not as fixed into the pattern of violence, interventions that reduce the level of dependency and bonding can be effective.

Why People Stay in Abusive Marriages

In discussing openly the reasons why someone might stay in an abusive marriage, people are often able to consider their own rationale for staying more realistically. This exploration, together with a clear appraisal of their current situation and a thoughtful review of the alternatives, can make them aware of their options.

Couples can discuss why a person might stay in an abusive relationship by considering the wife's point of view. She may have a number of beliefs that keep her in the relationship:

1. She may feel that her husband is ill and only she can take care of him.
2. She may feel that he might kill himself.
3. She may feel that he would never let her leave; he would come after her.

4. She may feel that the abuse is deserved or it is her fault.
5. She may fear that her parents would consider her a failure.
6. She may feel that separation and divorce are wrong.
7. She may feel that the children need their father.
8. She may not believe that she can survive without a man to support her.
9. She may believe that things will change for the better.
10. She may believe that this is the best she has a right to expect or that all marriages are like this.

It has also been noted that women with few resources for independent living are more likely to stay in abusive relationships. Often securing employment or going to a shelter, even for a short period of time, can introduce the element of choice into the relationship, upsetting the balance of power and, in turn, increasing the amount of abuse.

Exercise 38, Why Stay?, asks clients to discuss a situation they had trouble leaving in part A and to consider reasons why an abusive couple might stay together in part B.

Alternatives to Marriage

The purpose of discussing these issues is to introduce the element of choice, not to encourage couples to separate or to stay together. It is our bias that a relationship based on a realistic, deliberate decision to remain married is preferable to an unquestioning or nonvoluntary commitment.

Many times the possibility of divorce or marital separation is not actively and *realistically* considered. When the alternative of detaching and becoming single is approached, people often develop one of two opposing attitudes. First is to consider themselves without choice, or trapped. Second is to frequently think of divorce as a solution to all their problems and fantasize the state of divorce as one of freedom and bliss. The state of marriage is then unfavorably compared to an unrealistic fantasy. It is sometimes useful for clients to realistically consider what separation would mean for them.

Some of the areas clients need to think realistically about when they consider divorce are:

1. Informing family and friends of their decision;
2. Deciding who would move and where;
3. Arranging custody, support, and visitation if children are involved;
4. Continuing a relationship with the ex-spouse;

5. Preparing a budget;
6. Managing maintenance functions such as laundry, transportation, and food;
7. Re-entering the single world through dating and sex.

Exercise 39, Imagining Alternatives to Marriage, asks clients to think in a precise and detailed way about what divorce would mean to them. Frequently, some clients are in the early stages of separation. In a group setting, they can critique other clients' descriptions of what separation would be like. Even people who leave relationships that are quite abusive or dysfunctional experience the normal stages of grief. It can be instructive for other group members to witness this process. Again, the goal is not to moralize or encourage a particular decision, but to introduce a sense of choice and realism into the consideration of alternatives.

Contingency Plans

Contingency plans, plans made by the couple that outline what they will do should another episode of serious violence occur, can also reduce marital dependency. Often, couples with a history of violence have discussed what they would do if violence ever happened again. These discussions usually involve poorly reasoned threats to leave by the wife, which are not implemented. These idle threats have no capacity to serve as deterrents. The challenge, then, is for couples to develop contingency plans that are reasonable and practical and to discuss them in sufficient detail so that it becomes probable that they will be implemented. The discussion of these plans must convey, in a way that previous discussions have failed to, the seriousness of the intent to implement the contingency plan. Only if the couple is committed to the plan and believes that the plan will be implemented can the plan serve to deter subsequent violent episodes.

When formulating a contingency plan, the wife should consider exactly what level of threat, fear, or violence will make her leave the situation. This should involve detailing specific behaviors. She should also be very clear about exactly what she would do: who she would contact, where she would go, and so on. In some cases, it may be better for the wife not to specify exactly where she will go if this could endanger her safety. The husband can also fill out his portion of the Contingency Contract specifying what he will do and where he will go if violence occurs, thus eliminating the feeling the wife may have of being abandoned if he leaves to cool off after the violent incident.

Exercise 40, Contingency Plans, uses the Contingency Contract to help couples formulate contingency plans.

EXERCISE 32

PUTTING PRIMARY EMOTIONS INTO WORDS

Encourage clients to pay careful attention to their self-talk the next time they experience jealousy. The purpose is to identify the primary emotion and the thoughts that contribute to this feeling. Once identified, these primary thoughts and emotions should be put into words, thus short-circuiting the full-blown anger-fueled jealousy response.

For example, instead of saying "I am furious at you for dancing with someone else and it better not ever happen again" the client can try saying "I get worried when you dance with someone else, particularly if you look like you are enjoying it. Can we talk about it?"

EXERCISE 33

JEALOUSY ROLE REVERSAL

Describe to clients a situation that would be likely to arouse some level of jealousy without specifying the gender of the characters. For example:

> Your spouse mentions that he or she has been assigned a new co-worker of the opposite sex. The spouse has mentioned that the worker is attractive, and you notice that this person is discussed more and more frequently. About a week ago, the co-worker began calling in the evenings and talking with your spouse for several minutes. Although you try not to listen, you do overhear laughter.

First, have clients try to express how they would feel in the situation and have them role play how they would handle it. Then, have clients imagine that they are their spouse and are in the same situation. They are to think how their spouses would experience the co-worker calling and role play what their spouses are likely to feel and do.

EXERCISE 34

EXERCISING CONTROL

Ask clients to list all the different forms of control, surveillance, and detective work they could engage in if they were to give in completely to their jealousy. Encourage this brainstorming to include creative and exaggerated attempts, for example: tap the phone, record automobile mileage, forbid her to leave the house, don't permit any friendships with members of the opposite sex, don't let her get a job, don't permit looking at others, go through her pocketbook, open the mail. Then, inquire as to how effective they think their efforts would be.

EXERCISE 35

SEX ROLE CHARACTERISTICS

Ask clients to list under the headings Male and Female the stereotypical characteristics of each. As much as possible, try to link each description with its opposite. Example:

MALE	FEMALE
aggressive	passive
independent	dependent
tough	tender
nonemotional	emotional
competitive	cooperative
self-sufficient	needs others
not domestic	domestic
wants sex	wants romance
sexually active	sexually passive

After generating an extensive list, ask for clients' observations. Then ask them to disregard the headings and simply consider which attributes they consider desirable for themselves. They may conclude that it is desirable, for example, to be both tough and tender, both competitive and cooperative, both masculine and feminine.

EXERCISE 36

SEX ATTITUDES

Distribute the Sex Attitude Worksheet. Give participants a few minutes to complete it, and then discuss it, addressing any myths or inappropriate values that may be indicated.

EXERCISE 37

DECISION MAKING

A. Discuss the three methods of defining decision making, giving sufficient examples and opportunity for discussion so that the alternatives become clear to clients. Then ask them to vote or declare a preference for one of the three. It is important that the vote is in terms of preference rather than what they think others will expect of them.

B. Ask each client to read through the list of issues on the Decision Making Worksheet. Have couples work independently, following the instructions on the Worksheet. Then ask them to compare their results, paying particular attention to how they would like the decision making authority to be divided up (Xs). End the discussion of decision making by reinforcing areas of agreement and asking couples to apply their communication skills in an attempt to compromise on those areas of disagreement.

EXERCISE 38

WHY STAY?

A. Ask clients to think of a time they may have stayed in a situation well after it became apparent to them that they should probably leave. It may have been a job, school, the military, or living at home with parents. Now ask them to list all the factors that made it difficult to leave. Discuss.

EXERCISE 38 (cont.)

B. Ask clients to consider all the reasons why a couple might stay together in an abusive relationship. For the purpose of this exercise, adopt the point of view of the wife. Discuss which, if any, are valid or sufficient reasons.

EXERCISE 39

IMAGINING ALTERNATIVES TO MARRIAGE

Ask clients to think in a precise and detailed manner about what divorce would mean for them. Some areas to be included in their deliberations are: making the decision public, physical separation, child custody, support and visitation arrangements, relationship with ex-spouse, preparation of a budget, and maintenance functions.

EXERCISE 40

CONTINGENCY PLANS

Ask couples to think seriously about what they will do if violence or threatening acts begin again. Have them work independently to complete the Contingency Contract using the following questions and instructions:

What level of threat, fear, or violence would lead you to conclude that you must take serious action for your own welfare and the welfare of the other members of your family? Be as specific as possible in detailing what behaviors are not tolerable for you. This does not mean that you will consider anything less severe to be desirable or acceptable—just that this is your unquestioned limit. If the behaviors you detailed should occur, what action would you unfailingly (although perhaps reluctantly) choose to take? Include who you would contact, where you would go (if giving this information will not endanger you), how long you would stay, what support you would expect from your spouse, and what, if anything, might cause you to return.

SEX ATTITUDE WORKSHEET

Please read each of the following statements and write T for true if you mostly agree or F for false if you mostly disagree with the statement. This is for your own use and will *not* be collected.

_____ 1. Unless sex results in climax or orgasm it is a failure.

_____ 2. Sex equals intercourse. That is, any form of sexual interaction should follow this sequence: touch, arousal, erection, insertion, orgasm.

_____ 3. Sexual dissatisfactions and the inability to perform sexually are rare, occurring only in unhealthy relationships.

_____ 4. Masturbation is an inferior and immature form of sexual behavior.

_____ 5. The major factors in determining a woman's sexual response are the size of her partner's penis and how long he can last.

_____ 6. When an individual is in love and sexually satisfied, he or she is never sexually attracted to anybody else.

_____ 7. When couples are in love, there is no need to talk about sex because they automatically know how to please each other sexually.

_____ 8. All affectionate physical contact must lead to intercourse.

_____ 9. Sex is something that men do *to* women.

_____ 10. Sex is something that men do *for* women.

_____ 11. Men are always ready and willing to have sex.

_____ 12. Men should initiate all sexual activity.

_____ 13. Men should not express feelings of tenderness and affection.

_____ 14. Women should be more passive and less active when it comes to sex.

_____ 15. You should go along with your partner and have sex even if you are not interested at the moment.

DECISION MAKING WORKSHEET

Please read the following list. Make a check to the left of those decision issues that are most important to you. Draw a line through any
that do not apply. Add any items that you would like to include on
the list. Next, circle the answer that describes how decisions are
currently made in your family (1, 2, or 3). Finally, go back through
the list and draw an X through the alternative (1, 2, or 3) that expresses
how you *would like* decisions to be made.

	ALMOST ALWAYS HUSBAND	SHARED EQUALLY	ALMOST ALWAYS WIFE
_____ Where to live	1	2	3
_____ Whether wife works	1	2	3
_____ What job wife will take	1	2	3
_____ Whether to have children	1	2	3
_____ What church to go to	1	2	3
_____ How to handle finances	1	2	3
_____ What major purchases to make	1	2	3
_____ How to spend leisure time	1	2	3
_____ Who to socialize with	1	2	3
_____ When to have sex	1	2	3
_____ How to have sex	1	2	3
_____ How to discipline children	1	2	3
_____ What family activities to engage in	1	2	3
_____ When to visit relatives	1	2	3
_____ What job husband will take	1	2	3

Adapted from R. B. Stuart. *Marital pre-counseling inventory.* Champaign, Ill.: Research
Press, 1973.

CONTINGENCY CONTRACT

This contract represents the action I am fully prepared to take should the violent behavior specified occur. It should be understood that this is a statement of fact, not a threat. The action will be taken automatically. It will be taken because I believe that this is the proper response to violence and, ultimately, in the best interest of all of us.

WIFE

Should these behaviors occur: _____

_____

_____

_____

_____

I will always respond by: _____

_____

_____

_____

_____

HUSBAND

Should these behaviors occur: _____

_____

_____

_____

_____

I will always respond by: _____

_____

_____

_____

_____

SIGNED _____   _____
              Wife   Husband

Date _____

Chapter Ten

Closing the Program

The end of the program is naturally a time to review program content and have clients recommit themselves to eliminating spouse abuse. It is also important at this time to have clients examine their support networks, which will help them to remain free from spouse abuse after treatment has been terminated.

ISOLATION AND SOCIAL SUPPORT

A number of investigators have emphasized the importance of the absence of a support network in the dynamics of domestic violence. Justice and Justice (1976) cite several studies that found that the most striking difference between families in which child abuse occurred and families in which it did not had to do with the extent of associations outside the home. Lenowski (Note 12) compared abusing parents with a control group and reported that 81 percent of abusers as opposed to 43 percent of the nonabusers preferred to be alone, and almost 90 percent of the abusers did not have listed telephone numbers.

Straus (1977) reported that men who belonged to no organizations (clubs, lodges, or unions) had a higher rate of spouse abuse than a comparable group of men who belonged to organizations and experienced similar levels of stress. The same finding was reported for those regularly attending religious services as opposed to those who rarely attended.

If therapy is conducted in a group, participation in group discussions is an important step in reducing social isolation. Clients are able to relate to others who share their problem and have the opportunity to talk about intimate, important issues. Meaningful encounters, risks in self-disclosure, and reaching out to request or extend support are reinforced. A list of the names, addresses, and telephone numbers of all members should be distributed early in the program and contact outside the group setting encouraged. When problems such as transportation and babysitting are mentioned, the therapist may first see if others in the group are willing to provide assistance.

Typically, a feeling of general comfort and closeness between group members will have developed. Reinforce the idea that a few weeks ago the group members were all strangers, that there is nothing particularly unique about the composition of this group, and that if they were able to share and find some support here, it can also be experienced in other settings with other people. Encourage any spontaneous expressions of desire to meet informally as a support group in the future.

Clients' beliefs that might block free exchange of support include:

1. The belief that they must be totally self-sufficient.
2. A fear of imposing or making a nuisance of themselves.
3. The feeling that it is a sign of weakness to request help.
4. The concern that they will become obligated and open to being taken advantage of.

Often just discussing these issues openly and seeking clarification and feedback will serve to dispel them. Additionally, couples have been exposed to a number of influences during the course of treatment that may make it easier for them to ask for help. They discovered that they share a number of similarities with other couples involved in spouse abuse, and that although their involvement in violence may be somewhat unique, the content of their conflicts is the norm and not the exception. They have also had the opportunity to discuss and practice request making, and the influence of rigid sex role stereotypes and other attitudes that commonly inhibit asking for help has been diminished. It can also be easier for clients to ask for help if they understand that we all need other people to provide the five support functions that follow.

1. Listening. We need people who will simply listen without trying to solve the problem or telling us what we have been doing wrong.
2. Emotional support. We need people we can trust and confide in who will support us even when we are wrong.
3. Emotional challenge. In addition to support, we also need people who will not always agree; people whose judgment we respect, who can challenge us to grow.
4. Technical support. We need people who understand our work-related problems and can provide reinforcement in this area.
5. Technical challenge. We need people who can challenge, in addition to support, growth in work-related or other technical areas.

It is important for clients to recognize that their spouses cannot be expected to provide all of these support functions. For example, wives can provide listening, emotional support, and emotional challenge but unless they work or are trained in the same field as their husbands, they cannot provide technical support and challenge. A husband's desire to socialize with work colleagues, therefore, does not reflect badly on his wife.

Exercise 41, Strengthening Social Support, includes sections on strengthening friendships and support networks in parts A and B, finding out who provides support functions for clients in part C, encouraging clients to realize that no one is entirely self-sufficient in part D, and evaluating clients' support networks, using the Support Network Evaluation Worksheet, in part E.

PROGRAM REVIEW

It is important for clients to have the opportunity to demonstrate an increased willingness to assume personal responsibility for their behavior, to review positive accomplishments and potential problem areas, and to recommit themselves to eliminating domestic violence. This can be done by:

1. Reviewing the program content previously covered;
2. Consolidating the gains that the clients have achieved;
3. Anticipating and reviewing contingency plans for dealing with problems that may arise in the future; and
4. Renewing the commitment to maintain a violence-free home.

The Maintaining Your Gains form is used to enable clients to focus on positive accomplishments and acknowledge and reinforce their gains and those of their spouses. It is important that they give thought to section 4, the Danger Signals, which will indicate a return to previous, maladaptive styles of functioning. Possible warning signals may include: increasing consumption of alcohol, withdrawal, not putting negative content into words, working late, and arguing over the children. Again, these behaviors should be defined as warning signals, or cues, to review those coping strategies that have been found to be effective, rather than being defined as proof that the positive change accomplished was not real or in good faith.

An additional issue to be raised at this point is the personal consequences clients will experience should they fail to be successful in controlling anger and violence. An awareness of these adverse consequences can serve as a powerful deterrent. Clients should consider what the implications of another serious violent episode would be for them. Discussion of those implications can include the following points.

1. Legal action. Assault is a serious offense and charges are being brought by spouses and prosecuting attorneys in more and more cases.
2. Effects on the marriage. Although violence is often used in an attempt to control and keep a spouse, it often has the effect of driving her away.
3. Effects on children. As has frequently been discussed, children tend to model the behaviors to which they are exposed. Sufficient violence is likely to result in fearful, rebellious children who are more likely to engage in violence and abuse as adults.
4. Self-esteem. Most people are quite ashamed of their abusive behavior. Defensive efforts to justify such conduct are at best only partially successful.
5. Military career. For men in the military, administrative actions that may end their careers may be taken in cases of domestic violence.

The tone of the final session should be positive and optimistic. Serving some sort of special refreshments, distributing diplomas, and conducting a graduation ceremony can all contribute to creating this atmosphere. Clients should be encouraged to express their feelings about the program and, in group settings, their fellow group members. They should be told they are free to ask for additional help when needed, and asked for permission to recontact them at periodic intervals for follow-up evaluation. (A long-term evaluation form is included in the Appendix and may be copied for use in this program.)

It should be reinforced that clients are not expected to live "happily ever after," but that they now possess the skills to do something positive when the inevitable difficulties begin to occur. Eliminating violence is a *choice* that clients are free to make. They have acquired the skills necessary to achieve this, and there is no compelling reason why, with continued effort, they cannot accomplish it.

The Dyadic Adjustment Scale (Spanier, 1976) and the Locus of Control Scale (Nowicki & Marshall, 1974) can be administered during this final session. Clients' scores can be compared to their preprogram scores on the scales (if they were administered then) and used to assess clients' progress and evaluate the program. The Maintaining Your Gains form is used in this session to help clients review positive changes and commit themselves to continue with these changes. The Clients' Evaluation form requests candid and critical comments about the program from clients so the program can be refined and improved.

EXERCISE 41

STRENGTHENING SOCIAL SUPPORT

A. STRENGTHENING FRIENDSHIPS—Ask clients to call two friends during the week and simply talk for a couple of minutes. In a group setting, ask clients to call two other group members during the coming week.

B. STRENGTHENING SUPPORT NETWORKS—Ask clients to make a list of three different people who are important to them, and for each name write one thing that they could do to strengthen the relationship.

C. EXAMINING SUPPORT FUNCTIONS—Describe the five functions that people often need others to provide. Have clients write down the name of the person who provides the function for each. If any names occur more than twice, or if no one can be thought of to fulfill any particular function, the support network may require some attention.

D. REACHING OUT—Ask clients to think of all the things they might conceivably need help with and make a list. Encourage responses that indicate an awareness of the interdependency of family members and the fact that no one is entirely self-sufficient. Examples include: transportation, borrowing money, moving furniture, fixing the car, preparing the tax return, babysitting, cleaning the house, learning a new skill, and solving a personal problem.

Go through the list and ask clients to try to think of at least one person who could be asked to help with each need. Then ask them to consider which examples are easy and which are more difficult to ask for. Discuss the following:

1. What makes it hard to ask for help?
2. Are there differences between men and women in this area?
3. How do we feel about helping others?
4. What is the best way to ask for assistance?

E. EVALUATING SUPPORT NETWORKS—Distribute the Support Network Evaluation Worksheet and ask clients to complete it. Discuss the degree of isolation or connectedness reflected by each client's responses.

SUPPORT NETWORK EVALUATION WORKSHEET

Indicate with which of the following people you would be willing to discuss each topic. You may list more than one for each topic.

    A — Spouse
    B — Parent
    C — In-law
    D — Son or daughter
    E — Best friend
    F — Casual acquaintance
    G — Doctor
    H — Minister
    I — No one

_____ Marital difficulties you are having

_____ Concerns about your health

_____ Problems at work

_____ Something that hurt or embarrassed you

_____ Something you worry about or are afraid of

_____ Details of your sex life

_____ Financial problems

_____ Problems with your children

_____ An accomplishment or something you are proud of

_____ Something you need help with

_____ Something you did wrong as a child

_____ Your participation in this program

_____ Something you cried about

MAINTAINING YOUR GAINS WORKSHEET

What positive changes have you noticed in yourself, in your spouse, and in your relationship since starting treatment?

_____

_____

What things do you think have led to those positive changes? Are there things that you have learned or are doing differently that are especially helpful to you?

_____

_____

Are there any problems that may occur again that you need to be particularly aware of? If so, what are the danger signals that alert you to these problems?

_____

_____

What are your best ways of coping with these problems if they occur again?

_____

_____

What additional changes are you or you and your spouse committed to make?

_____

_____

What date (in about 2 months) will you review your gains, review the treatment contents, and renew your Client's Contract? _____

SIGNED _____

_____ Therapist

_____ Date

CLIENT'S EVALUATION

Date ――――――――――   Therapist ――――――――――

Place ――――――――――――――――――――

For the following three questions, please circle the numbers that best describe how you feel.

1. *How did you feel about the treatment?*

Not useful	1	2	3	4	5	6	Useful
Too short	1	2	3	4	5	6	Too long
Not understandable	1	2	3	4	5	6	Understandable
Too simple	1	2	3	4	5	6	Too complex

2. *How did you feel about the therapist?*

Discouraged participation	1	2	3	4	5	6	Encouraged participation
Unprepared	1	2	3	4	5	6	Prepared
Unfriendly	1	2	3	4	5	6	Friendly
Unclear	1	2	3	4	5	6	Clear
Unskilled	1	2	3	4	5	6	Skilled

3. *What was your overall reaction?*

Not involved	1	2	3	4	5	6	Involved
Learned nothing	1	2	3	4	5	6	Learned a lot
Did not enjoy	1	2	3	4	5	6	Enjoyed
Not interested	1	2	3	4	5	6	Interested

4. What was the most beneficial part of the program to you? ―――――

――――――――――――――――――――

――――――――――――――――――――

――――――――――――――――――――

5. What was the least beneficial part to you? ――――――――――

――――――――――――――――――――

――――――――――――――――――――

――――――――――――――――――――

CLIENT'S EVALUATION (cont.)

6. What changes would you suggest in the program? _____

_____

_____

_____

7. Do you have any additional comments you would like to make?

_____

_____

_____

Appendix

INTAKE INTERVIEW

IDENTIFYING INFORMATION: HUSBAND

Name _____

Address _____

Home telephone no. _____ Work telephone no. _____

Date of birth _____ Race _____

Last grade completed in school _____

Social Security no. _____ Occupation _____

Length of time at present job _____

How stressful is present job?

   Not at all   Slightly stressful   Stressful   Very stressful   N/A

All things considered, how satisfied are you with your job?

   Very unsatisfied   Unsatisfied   Satisfied   Very satisfied   N/A

Are you a combat veteran?

   Yes   No

Length of time in service, if any _____

Number of previous marriages, if any _____

Age at time of first marriage _____

How long have you been married this time? _____

Are you and your wife:

   Living together   Separated   Divorced

IDENTIFYING INFORMATION: WIFE

Name _____

Address _____

Home telephone no. _____   Work telephone no. _____

Date of birth _____   Race _____

Last grade completed in school _____

Social Security no. _____   Occupation _____

Length of time at present job _____

How stressful is present job?

    Not at all   Slightly stressful   Stressful   Very stressful   N/A

All things considered, how satisfied are you with your job?

    Very unsatisfied   Unsatisfied   Satisfied   Very satisfied   N/A

Number of previous marriages, if any _____

Age at time of first marriage _____

How long have you been married this time? _____

BACKGROUND INFORMATION: HUSBAND

- Were you raised primarily by:

    Mother & father   Father only   Father & stepmother

    Mother only   Mother & stepfather   Grandparents

    Other family   Foster family

- During the time you were growing up did your father (or adult male) —

Comfort or help you when you had troubles?

    Never   Sometimes   Often   Almost always   N/A

Hit or slap you?

    Never   Sometimes   Often   Almost always   N/A

Scold or yell at you?

    Never   Sometimes   Often   Almost always   N/A

Beat you?

Never   Sometimes   Often   Almost always   N/A

If beaten, describe the beatings. _____

_____

_____

_____

_____

- During the time that you were growing up did your mother (or adult female) —

Comfort or help you when you had troubles?

Never   Sometimes   Often   Almost always   N/A

Hit or slap you?

Never   Sometimes   Often   Almost always   N/A

Scold or yell at you?

Never   Sometimes   Often   Almost always   N/A

Beat you?

Never   Sometimes   Often   Almost always   N/A

If beaten, describe the beatings. _____

_____

_____

_____

_____

- How old were you the last time you were spanked or hit by a parent?

3 or younger   3-6   6-12   12-15   15-18   Older than 18

- Looking back, do you consider yourself to have been punished too severely?

Yes   Maybe   No

Punished unfairly?

Yes   Maybe   No

Physically or emotionally abused?

Yes   Maybe   No

- Did you ever see or hear the people who raised you argue or fight?

Never   Sometimes   Often   Very often

- Did you ever see or hear your father hit your mother?

Never   Sometimes   Often   Very often   N/A

- Did you ever see or hear your mother hit your father?

Never   Sometimes   Often   Very often   N/A

- When you were growing up, were you ever afraid of being physically harmed?

Never   Sometimes   Often   Very often

BACKGROUND INFORMATION: WIFE

- Were you raised primarily by:

Mother & father   Father only   Father & stepmother

Mother only   Mother & stepfather   Grandparents

Other family   Foster family

- During the time you were growing up did your father (or adult male) —

Comfort or help you when you had troubles?

Never   Sometimes   Often   Almost always   N/A

Hit or slap you?

Never   Sometimes   Often   Almost always   N/A

Scold or yell at you?

Never   Sometimes   Often   Almost always   N/A

Beat you?

Never   Sometimes   Often   Almost always   N/A

If beaten, describe the beatings. _____

_____

_____

_____

_____

● During the time that you were growing up did your mother (or adult female) —

Comfort or help you when you had troubles?

    Never   Sometimes   Often   Almost always   N/A

Hit or slap you?

    Never   Sometimes   Often   Almost always   N/A

Scold or yell at you?

    Never   Sometimes   Often   Almost always   N/A

Beat you?

    Never   Sometimes   Often   Almost always   N/A

If beaten, describe the beatings. _____

_____

_____

_____

_____

● How old were you the last time you were spanked or hit by a parent?

    3 or younger   3-6   6-12   12-15   15-18   Older than 18

● Looking back, do you consider yourself to have been punished too severely?

    Yes   Maybe   No

Punished unfairly?

    Yes   Maybe   No

Physically or emotionally abused?

    Yes   Maybe   No

- Did you ever see or hear the people who raised you argue or fight?

    Never   Sometimes   Often   Very often

- Did you ever see or hear your father hit your mother?

    Never   Sometimes   Often   Very often   N/A

- Did you ever see or hear your mother hit your father?

    Never   Sometimes   Often   Very often   N/A

- When you were growing up, were you ever afraid of being physically harmed?

    Never   Sometimes   Often   Very often

VIOLENCE HISTORY: HUSBAND AND WIFE

Now I would like to learn about the violence in your relationship. I am going to ask each of you the same questions. You may find that you agree or that you remember things differently. (If only one spouse is present, mark all responses for the absent spouse as N/A.)

- The first time there was any violence in your relationship were you:

    1 — Going together   2 — Just married

    3 — Married less than 1 year   4 — Married more than 1 year

    Husband _____   Wife _____

- How upset were you about the first incident of violence when it happened?

    1 — Not upset   2 — Slightly upset   3 — Upset

    4 — Very upset

    H _____   W _____

    Did you tend to blame yourself?

    1 — Yes   2 — No

    H _____   W _____

    Blame your spouse?

    1 — Yes   2 — No

    H _____   W _____

Blame someone or something else?

    1 — Yes   2 — No

H _____   W _____

If you blamed someone or something else, specify.

H _____

_____

W _____

_____

- Have either of you ever been involved in physical violence in a previous marriage or relationship?

    1 — Yes   2 — No

H _____   W _____

If so, describe.

H _____

_____

_____

_____

W _____

_____

_____

_____

- Have you ever used weapons or objects as weapons against another person?

    1 — Yes   2 — No   3 — A member of your family

H _____   W _____

- When did your last incident of violence happen?

H _____   W _____

Describe the incident.

H _____

_____

_____

_____

W _____

_____

_____

_____

- What sort of injuries did you receive?

    1 — None   2 — Minor, no treatment needed

    3 — Moderate, treatment needed

    4 — Serious, hospitalization needed

    5 — Permanent disability

    H _____   W _____

- Did any of the following get involved at the time of the incident?

    1 — No one   2 — Law officers   3 — Neighbors

    4 — Other family members   5 — Medical personnel

    6 — Counselors   7 — Minister or priest

    8 — Friends   9 — Others

    H _____   W _____

    Did any of these people refer you to this program?

    H _____   W _____

    Did any of these people discuss your problems with violence with you?

    H _____   W _____

- How upset were you after the last incident of violence?

    1 — Not upset   2 — Slightly upset

    3 — Upset   4 — Very upset

    H _____   W _____

- After the last incident of violence, did you tend to blame yourself?

    1 — Yes   2 — No

    H _____   W _____

    Blame your spouse?

    1 — Yes   2 — No

    H _____   W _____

    Blame someone or something else?

    1 — Yes   2 — No

    H _____   W _____

    If you blamed someone or something else, specify:

    H _____

    _____

    W _____

    _____

- Have you ever had problems outside of the home with anger or violence?

    1 — No   2 — Some   3 — Several times

    H _____   W _____

    If so, specify how.

    H _____

    _____

    _____

    _____

W _____

_____

_____

_____

● Have you ever been arrested?.

    1 — No

    2 — As a juvenile, nonviolent charge

    3 — As an adult, nonviolent charge

    4 — As a juvenile or an adult, violent charge

    H _____   W _____

● Had you been drinking or using drugs at the time of the last incident of violence?

    1 — No   2 — Some alcohol

    3 — A lot of alcohol   4 — Drugs

    H _____   W _____

● Do you feel that alcohol or drugs contribute to your marital problems?

    1 — Yes   2 — Maybe   3 — No

    H _____   W _____

● Do you feel that your spouse has an alcohol or drug problem?

    1 — Yes   2 — Maybe   3 — No

    H _____   W _____

● How often do you feel frightened at home?

    1 — Never   2 — Sometimes   3 — Often   4 — Almost always

    H _____   W _____

SOCIAL INFORMATION: HUSBAND AND WIFE

● What is your religion?

    H _____   W _____.

How important is your religion to you?

    1 — Not at all   2 — Slightly important

    3 — Important   4 — Very important

H _____   W _____

- How often do you go out to socialize or to have fun with your spouse?

    1 — less than 1 time per month   2 — 1 time per month

    3 — 1 time every 2 weeks   4 — 1 time per week

    5 — 2 to 4 times per week   6 — Almost every night

H _____   W _____

Without your spouse?

H _____   W _____

FAMILY INFORMATION: HUSBAND AND WIFE

- How many of each of the following live in your home?

    Children under 5 _____

    Children 6 to 10 _____

    Children older than 10 _____

    Children who are physically or mentally disabled _____

    Stepchildren   H _____   W _____

    Other adults _____

- Do you think that the children have been affected by the conflict and violence in your home?

    1 — No   2 — Slightly   3 — Moderately

    4 — Greatly   5 — N/A

H _____   W _____

- Do you usually agree with your spouse when it comes to disciplining the children?

    1 — Yes   2 — No   3 — N/A

H _____   W _____

- How do you feel about the way that your spouse disciplines the children?

    1 — Too easy   2 — Just about right

    3 — Somewhat too harsh   4 — Much too harsh   5 — N/A

    H _____   W _____

- How do you feel about the way that you discipline the children?

    1 — Too easy   2 — Just about right

    3 — Somewhat too harsh   4 — Much too harsh   5 — N/A

    H _____   W _____

    Would you like some help with parenting such as individual counseling or parenting classes?

    1 — Yes   2 — No

    H _____   W _____

- Would you like some help with how to control anger and violence in your marriage?

    1 — Yes   2 — No

    H _____   W _____

- Will you be attending treatment?

    1 — Yes   2 — No

    H _____   W _____

    If not, explain.

    H _____

    _____

    W _____

    _____

- Additional observations _____

    _____

    _____

    _____

Present at interview

    Husband only   Wife only   Both

Date of interview _____

Name of interviewer _____

LONG-TERM EVALUATION

Name _____

Telephone no. _____ Date _____

Interviewer _____

1. This is (your name) calling from the (treatment center).
   (therapist's name) asked me to call and see how you are doing.
   Is this a good time to talk? It will take only a minute. (If yes,
   go to part 3.)

2. When can I call you back? _____

   _____

   Thank you.

3. Have you and your spouse had any more problems with violence?

   Yes   No

   (If no, go to part 4.)

   How many incidents of violence have you had?   _____

   _____

   Do you consider the incident(s):

   Minor   Moderately serious   Serious

   Was anyone injured?

   Yes   No

   If so, who?

   Husband   Wife   Both   Other person

   If injuries were received, what sort were they?

   Minor, no treatment needed

   Moderate, treatment needed

   Serious, hospitalization needed

   Permanent disability

Were the police notified?

Yes   No

If so, by whom?

Husband   Wife   Other

4. Did you and your spouse both participate in the treatment?

Yes   Husband only   Wife only

Did it help you?

Yes   No

Did it help your spouse? (Ask even if spouse did not attend.)

Yes   No

Did it help your marriage?

Yes   No

5. Is there any other way that we can be of help to you?

Yes   No

If so, how? _____

_____

Thank you.

Reference Notes

1. Neidig, P.H., Friedman, D.H., & Collins, B.S. *Attitudinal charac-teristics of men who have engaged in spouse abuse.* Paper presented at the Second National Conference for Family Violence Researchers, Durham, N.H., 1984. (Available from Behavioral Science Associates, PO Box 1485, Beaufort, S.C. 29901).

2. Neidig, P.H., Friedman, D.H., & Collins, B.S. *The violence continuum: A conceptual model of spouse abuse with treatment implications.* Manuscript submitted for publication, 1984. (Available from Behavioral Science Associates, PO Box 1485, Beaufort, S.C. 29901).

3. Neidig, P.H., Friedman, D.H., & Howell, W.L. *Spouse abuse intervention program in the military setting.* Unpublished manuscript, 1983. (Available from Behavioral Science Associates, PO Box 1485, Beaufort, S.C. 29901).

4. Friedman, D.H. *Preliminary research findings.* Unpublished manuscript, 1983. (Available from Behavioral Science Associates, PO Box 1485, Beaufort, S.C. 29901).

5. Coleman, D.H., & Straus, M. *Alcohol abuse and family violence.* Unpublished manuscript, University of New Hampshire, 1981.

6. Neidig, P.H. *Spouse abuse: The causal model with assessment procedures.* Unpublished manuscript, 1984. (Available from Behavioral Science Associates, PO Box 1485, Beaufort, S.C. 29901).

7. Yllo, K.A. *The status of women and wife beating in the U.S.: A multi-level analysis.* Unpublished doctoral dissertation, University of New Hampshire, 1980.

8. Friedman, D.H. *Locus of control, self-esteem and dogmatism in male marine spouse abusers.* Unpublished manuscript, 1982. (Available from Behavioral Science Associates, PO Box 1485, Beaufort, S.C. 29901).

9. Ganley, A., & Harris, L. *Domestic violence: Issues in designing and implementing programs for male batterers.* Paper presented at the Annual Meeting of the American Psychological Association, Toronto, 1978.

10. Shwed, J.A., & Straus, M. *The military environment and child abuse.* Unpublished manuscript, University of New Hampshire, 1979.

11. Neidig, P.H. *Stress management manual.* Unpublished manuscript, 1982. (Available from Behavioral Science Associates, PO Box 1485, Beaufort, S.C. 29901).

12. Lenowski, E.F. *Translating injury data into preventive services—Physical child abuse.* Unpublished manuscript, 1973. (Available from Division of Emergency Medicine, University of Southern California Medical Center, Los Angeles, Calif. 90033).

References

Alberti, R., & Emmons, M. *Your perfect right.* San Luis Obispo: Impact Publishers, 1970.

Averill, J.R. An analysis of psycho-physical symbolism and its influence on theories of emotion. *Journal for the Theory of Social Behavior,* 1974, *4,* 147–190.

Bach, G.R. A theory of intimate aggression. *Psychological Reports,* 1963, *12,* 449–450.

Bagarozzi, D.A., & Giddings, C.W. A conceptual model for understanding and treating marital violence. *ARETE,* 1982, *8,*322–334.

Bagarozzi, D.A., & Wordarski, J.S. A social exchange typology of conjugal relationships and conflict development. *Journal of Marriage and Family Counseling,* 1977, *3,* 53–60.

Balswick, J.O., & Peek, C.W. The inexpressive male: A tragedy of American society. *The Family Coordinator,* October 1971, pp. 363–368.

Bandura, A. Learning and behavioral theories of aggression. In I.L. Kutash, S.B. Kutash, L.B. Schlesinger, & Associates (Eds.), *Violence: Perspectives on murder and aggression.* San Francisco: Jossey-Bass, 1978.

Bandura, A., & Walters, R.H. *Source learning and personality development.* New York: Holt, Rinehart, & Winston, 1963.

Beck, A.T. *Cognitive therapy and emotional disorders.* New York: New American Library, 1979.

Bem, S.L. Bem sex role inventory. In C.G. Carney & S.L. McMahon (Eds.), *Exploring contemporary male/female roles.* San Diego: University Associates, 1977. (a)

Bem, S.L. Beyond androgeny: Some presumptuous prescriptions for a liberated sexual identity. In C.G. Carney & S.L. McMahon (Eds.), *Exploring contemporary male/female roles: A facilitator's guide.* San Diego: University Associates, 1977. (b)

Berk, R.A., Berk, S.F., Loseke, D.R., & Rauma, D. Mutual combat and other family violence myths. In D. Finkelhor, R.J. Gelles, G.T. Hotaling, & M.A. Straus (Eds.), *The dark side of families: Current family violence research.* Beverly Hills, Calif.: Sage Publications, 1983.

Berkowitz, L. Experimental investigation of hostility catharsis. *Journal of Consulting and Clinical Psychology,* 1970, *35,* 1–7.

Bernstein, D.A., & Borkovec, T.D. *Progressive relaxation training: A manual for the helping professions.* Champaign, Ill.: Research Press, 1973.

Borkovec, T.D., Grayson, J.B., & Cooper, K.M. Treatment of general tension: Subjective and physiological effects of progressive relaxation. *Journal of Consulting and Clinical Psychology,* 1978, *46,* 518–528.

Borkovec, T.D., & Sides, J.K. Critical procedural variables related to the physiological effects of progressive relaxation: A review. *Behaviour Research and Therapy,* 1979, *17,* 119–125.

Burns, D.D. *Feeling good: The new mood therapy.* New York: William Morrow, 1980.

Chandler, M.J. Egocentrism and antisocial behavior: The assessment and training of social perspective–taking skills. *Developmental Psychology,* 1973, *9,* 326–332.

Constantine, L.L. Jealousy from theory to intervention. In D. Olsen (Ed.), *Treating relationships.* Lake Mills, Iowa: Graphic, 1976.

Davis, M., Eshelman, E.R., & McKay, M. *The relaxation and stress reduction workbook.* Richmond, Calif.: New Harbinger, 1980.

Didato, S.V. *Psychotechniques.* New York: Playboy Paperbacks, 1980.

Dobash, R.E., & Dobash, R. *Violence against wives: The case against patriarchy.* New York: The Free Press, 1979.

Ellis, A. *Reason and emotion in psychotherapy.* New York: Lyle Stuart, 1962.

Ellis, A. *How to live with—and without—anger.* New York: Thomas Crowell, 1977.

Farber, L.H. *Lying, despair, jealousy, envy, sex, suicide, drugs, and the good life.* New York: Basic Books, 1976.

Feshbach, S. The function of aggression and the regulation of aggressive drive. *Psychological Review,* 1964, *103,* 119–131.

Geller, J. Reaching the battered husband. *Social Work with Groups,* 1978, *1,* 27–37.

Gelles, R. *The violent home: A study of physical aggression between husbands and wives.* Beverly Hills, Calif.: Sage Publications, 1972.

Gelles, R., & Straus, M.A. Determinants of violence in the family: Toward a theoretical integration. In W.R. Burr, R. Hill, F.I. Nye, & I.L. Reiss (Eds.), *Contemporary theories about the family.* New York: Free Press, 1979.

Goldberg, H. *The hazards of being male: Surviving the myth of masculine privilege.* New York: New American Library, Signet, 1976.

Goode, W.J. Force and violence in the family. *Journal of Marriage and the Family,* 1971, *33,* 624–636.

Gottman, J., Notarius, C., Gonso, J., & Markman, H. *A couple's guide to communication.* Champaign, Ill.: Research Press, 1976.

Guerney, B.G. *Relationship enhancement.* San Francisco: Jossey-Bass, 1977.

Harrell, J., & Guerney, B. Training married couples in conflict negotiation skills. In D. Olsen (Ed.), *Treating relationships.* Lake Mills, Iowa: Graphic, 1976.

Holmes, T.H., & Rahe, R.H. The social readjustment rating scale. *Journal of Psychosomatic Research,* 1967, *11,* 213–218.

Jacobson, E. *Progressive relaxation: A physiological and clinical investigation of muscular states and their significance in psychology and medical practice.* Chicago: University of Chicago Press, 1938.

Jacobson, N.S., & Margolin, G. *Marital therapy: Strategies based on social learning and behavior exchange principles.* New York: Brunner/Mazel, 1979.

Jakubowski, P.A. Assertive behavior and clinical problems of women. In E.I. Rawlings & D.K. Carter (Eds.), *Psychotherapy for Women*. Springfield, Ill.: Charles C. Thomas, 1977.

Jakubowski, P.A., & Lange, A.J. *The assertive option: Your rights and responsibilities*. Champaign, Ill.: Research Press, 1978.

James, W. What is emotion? *Mind*, 1884, *9*, 188–204.

Justice, B., & Justice, R. *The abusing family*. New York: Human Sciences Press, 1976.

Kelly, C. Assertion theory. In J.W. Pfeiffer & J.E. Jones (Eds.), *1976 annual handbook for group facilitators*. San Diego: University Associates, 1976.

Kelly, G. *The psychology of personal constructs*. New York: Norton, 1955.

LaBell, L.S. Wife abuse: A sociological study of battered women and their mates. *Victimology: An International Journal*, 1979, *4*, 257–267.

Leyens, J.P., Cisneros, T., & Hossay, J.F. Decentration as a means for reducing aggression after exposure to violent stimuli. *European Journal of Social Psychology*, 1976, *6*, 459–473.

Margolin, G. Conjoint marital therapy to enhance anger management and reduce spouse abuse. *American Journal of Family Therapy*, 1979, *7* (2), 13–24.

Martin, D. *Battered wives*. New York: Simon & Schuster, Pocket Books, 1976.

Medina, C. Loss of childhood as a factor in domestic violence. In *Hispanic report of families and youth*. Washington, D.C.: The National Coalition of Hispanics Mental Health Organization, 1981.

Mehrabian, A., & Epstein, N. A measure of emotional empathy. *Journal of Personality*, 1972, *40*, 525–543.

Meichenbaum, D. *Cognitive behavior modification*. New York: Plenum, 1977.

Miller, S., Wackman, D., Nunnally, E., & Saline, C. *Straight talk: A new way to get closer to others by saying what you really mean*. New York: New American Library, 1981.

Morse, D.R., & Furst, M.L. *Stress for success.* New York: Van Nostrand Reinhold, 1979.

Mouton, J.S., & Blake, R.R. *The marriage grid.* New York: McGraw-Hill, 1971.

Mulvihill, D.J., Tumin, M.M., & Curtis, L.A. *Crimes of violence: Staff report to the National Commission on the Causes and Prevention of Violence.* Washington, D.C.: U.S. Government Printing Office, 1969.

Neidig, P.H. Women's shelters, men's collectives and other issues in the field of spouse abuse. *Victimology: An International Journal,* in press.

Novaco, R.W. *Anger control.* Lexington, Mass.: Lexington Books, 1975.

Novaco, R.W. The functions and the regulation of the arousal of anger. *American Journal of Psychiatry,* 1976, *133,* 1124–1128.

Novaco, R.W. *Anger and coping with provocation: An instructional manual.* Irvine, Calif.: University of California Press, 1977.

Novaco, R.W. Anger and coping with stress: Cognitive behavioral interventions. In J.P. Foreyt & D.P. Rathsen (Eds.), *Cognitive behavior therapy: Research and applications.* New York: Plenum, 1978.

Nowicki, S., Jr., & Marshall, D. A locus of control scale for college as well as non-college adults. *Journal of Personality Assessment,* 1974, *38,* 136–137.

Nowinski, J. *Becoming satisfied: A man's guide to sexual fulfillment.* Englewood Cliffs, N.J.: Prentice-Hall, 1980.

Pagelow, M.D. *Woman battering: Victims and their experiences.* Beverly Hills, Calif.: Sage Publications, 1981.

Parsons, T. Certain primary sources and patterns of aggression in the social structure of the Western world. *Psychiatry,* 1947, *10,* 67–81.

Pfouts, J.H. Violent families: Coping responses of abused wives. *Child Welfare,* 1978, *57,* 101–111.

Rimm, D.C., Hill, G.A., Brown, N.N., & Stuart, J.E. Group-assertive training in treatment of expression of inappropriate anger. *Psychological Reports,* 1974, *34,* 791–798.

Rosenbaum, A., & O'Leary, K.D. Marital violence: Characteristics of abusive couples. *Journal of Consulting and Clinical Psychology,* 1981, *49,* 63–71.

Rounsaville, B.J. Theories in marital violence: Evidence from a study of battered women. *Victimology: An International Journal,* 1978, *3,* 11–31.

Russell, R.K., & Gribble, M.W. Progressive muscle relaxation: Appropriate and inappropriate applications. In P.A. Keller & L.G. Ritt (Eds.), *Innovations in clinical practice: A source book.* Sarasota, Fla.: Professional Resources Exchange, 1982.

Saunders, D.G. Counseling the violent husband. In P.A. Keller & L.G. Ritt (Eds.), *Innovations in clinical practice: A source book.* Sarasota, Fla.: Professional Resources Exchange, 1982.

Schacter, S., & Singer, J.E. Cognitive social and physiological determinants of emotional states. *Psychological Review,* 1962, *69,* 379–399.

Sears, R., Maccoby, E., & Levin, H. *Patterns of childrearing.* New York: Harper and Row, 1957.

Selye, H. *Stress without distress.* New York: New American Library, 1974.

Shapiro, R.J. Therapy with violent families. In S. Saunders, A.M. Anderson, C.A. Hart, & G.M. Rubenstein (Eds.), *Violent individuals and families.* Springfield, Ill.: Charles C. Thomas, 1984.

Singer, D.L. Aggression arousal, hostile humor and catharsis. *Journal of Personality and Social Psychology Monograph,* 1968, *8* (1, Pt. 2).

Snell, J.E., Rosenwald, R.J., & Robey, A. The wifebeater's wife. *Archives of General Psychiatry,* 1964, *11,* 107–112.

Spanier, G.B. Measuring dyadic adjustment: New scales for assessing the quality of marriage and similar dyads. *Journal of Marriage and the family,* 1976, *38,* 15–28.

Spence, J.J., & Helmreich, R.L. *Masculinity and femininity: Their psychological dimensions, correlates, and antecedents.* Austin, Tex.: University of Texas Press, 1978.

Sprey, J. The family as a system in conflict. *Journal of Marriage and the Family,* 1969, *31,* 699–706.

Steinmetz, S.K., & Straus, M.A. (Eds.). *Violence in the family.* New York: Dodd, Mead, 1974.

Straus, M.A. A sociological perspective on the prevention and treatment of wife beating. In M. Roy (Ed.), *Battered women: A psychosociological study of domestic violence.* New York: Van Nostrand Reinhold, 1977 .

Straus, M.A. Measuring intrafamily conflict and violence: The conflict tactics scales. *Journal of Marriage and the Family,* 1979, *41,* 75–88.

Straus, M.A. Social stress and marital violence in a national sample of American families. *Annals of the New York Academy of Science,* 1980, *347,* 229–250. (a)

Straus, M.A. Victims and aggressors in marital violence. *American Behavioral Scientist,* 1980, *23,* 681–704. (b)

Straus, M.A., Gelles, R.H., & Steinmetz, S.K. *Behind closed doors: Violence in the American family.* New York: Doubleday/Anchor, 1981.

Stuart, R.B. *Marital pre-counseling inventory.* Champaign, Ill.: Research Press, 1972.

Stuart, R.B. *Helping couples change: Clinical demonstrations.* New York: BMA Audio Cassettes, 1980. (Audiotape) (a)

Stuart, R.B. *Helping couples change: A social learning approach to marital therapy.* New York: Guilford Press, 1980. (b)

Surgeon General's Scientific Advisory Committee on Television and Social Behavior. *Television and growing up: The impact of televised violence.* Rockville, Md.: U.S. Department of Health, Education, and Welfare, 1971.

Sykes, G.M., & Matza, D. Techniques of neutralization: A theory of delinquency. *American Sociological Review,* 1957, *22,* 664–670.

Tavris, C. *Anger: The misunderstood emotion.* New York: Simon & Schuster, 1982.

Teismann, M.W. Jealousy: Systematic problem-solving therapy with couples. *Family Process,* 1979, *18,* 151–160.

Tolby, J. Violence and the masculine ideal: Some qualitative data. *The Annals of the American Academy of Political and Social Science,* 1966, *364,* 19–27.

Tyler, C.W. Violence as a public health problem: Is there a role for health promotion and education? *Health Education Focal Points,* August 1983, pp. 1–3.

Walker, L. *The battered woman.* New York: Harper and Row, 1979.

Walker, L. A feminist perspective on domestic violence. In R. Stuart (Ed.), *Violent behavior: Social learning approaches to prediction, management and treatment.* New York: Brunner/Mazel, 1981.

Walker, L. The battered woman syndrome study. In D. Finkelhor, R.J. Gelles, G.T. Hotaling, & M.A. Straus (Eds.), *The dark side of families: Current family violence research.* Beverly Hills, Calif.: Sage Publications, 1983.

Walters, R.H. Implications of laboratory studies of aggression for the control and regulation of violence. *The Annals of the American Academy of Political and Social Science,* 1966, *364,* 60–72.

Watzlawick, P., Beavin, J., & Jackson, D. *Pragmatics of human communication.* New York: Norton, 1967.

Weitzman, J., & Dreen, K. Wife beating: A view of the marital dyad. *Social Casework: The Journal of Contemporary Social Work,* May 1982, pp. 259–265.

West, L., Turner, W., & Dunwoody, E. *Wife abuse in the armed forces.* Washington, D.C.: Center for Women Policy Studies, 1981.

Whitehurst, R. Violently jealous husbands. *Sexual Behavior,* 1971, *4,* 32–38.

Wiest, J. Treatment of violent offenders. *Clinical Social Work Journal,* 1981, *9,* 271–281.

Wolfgang, M.E. *Patterns in criminal homicide.* Philadelphia: University of Pennsylvania Press, 1958.

Zais, M., & Taylor, W. Stress and the military. In S.P. Day (Ed.), *Life stress* (Vol. 3). New York: Van Nostrand Reinhold, 1982.

Zilbergeld, B. *Male sexuality: A guide to sexual fulfillment.* Boston: Little, Brown, 1978.

About the Authors

Peter H. Neidig and **Dale H. Friedman** are partners in Behavioral Science Associates, Inc., a social service consulting firm in Beaufort, South Carolina. For the past 3 years, they have been conducting research in the area of domestic violence and providing treatment for couples involved in abusive relationships. They have conducted workshops throughout the country on the prevention and treatment of spouse abuse.

Peter H. Neidig received his Ph.D. in Clinical Psychology from the University of Tennessee in 1970. Since then he has served on the faculty of Western Illinois University and the University of South Carolina and is currently the Director of Consultation and Education at Coastal Empire Mental Health Center in Beaufort, South Carolina. He maintains a private clinical practice.

Dale H. Friedman received an M.S. in Health Education from the University of Washington in 1982. The treatment program outlined in this book was initially based on research done for her master's thesis. For the past 3 years she has worked at Coastal Empire Mental Health Center developing and conducting prevention and education programs. She now devotes full time to administering Behavioral Science Associates, Inc. programs.